⭐ GREAT IRISH SPORTS STARS

SONIA O'SULLIVAN

NATASHA MAC A'BHÁIRD is a freelance writer and editor. Her first two children's books, *Missing Ellen* and *Olanna's Big Day,* were both chosen for the White Ravens Collection. She is the author of ten books for children, including the *Star Club* series, *My Ireland Activity* series and *Reindeer Down.*

Natasha didn't play many sports as a child, but has now found an outlet for running around through parkrun. She also loves supporting the Donegal GAA and Republic of Ireland soccer teams and her daughters' teams. Having grown up watching the highs and lows of Sonia O'Sullivan's running career, she was thrilled to have the opportunity to tell her story.

GREAT IRISH SPORTS STARS

SONIA O'SULLIVAN

Natasha Mac a'Bháird

THE O'BRIEN PRESS
DUBLIN

First published 2020 by
The O'Brien Press Ltd,
12 Terenure Road East, Rathgar,
Dublin 6, Ireland
D06 HD27
Tel: +353 1 4923333; Fax: +353 1 4922777
E-mail: books@obrien.ie.
Website: www.obrien.ie
The O'Brien Press is a member of Publishing Ireland.

ISBN: 978-1-78849-207-2

8 7 6 5 4 3 2 1
23 22 21 20

Printed in the UK by Clays Ltd, Elcograf S.p.A.
The paper in this book is produced using pulp from managed forests.

Published in:

CONTENTS

CHAPTER ONE

SUNNY DAYS IN COBH

The sun shone down on Wilmount Park in Cobh as the local kids met up in their usual spot.

Sonia loved nothing more than being out in the fresh air with a big gang of friends. Those long summer evenings when they had nowhere to be and nothing to do but play for hours on end. They were ten years old and they hadn't a care in the world.

'What'll we play?' Catherine asked.

'Hide and seek!' suggested Deirdre.

Deirdre said she'd be seeker, and the rest of the gang spread out, running in all different directions, finding hiding places behind cars and bushes and around corners.

Sonia hid in a garden, crouching down behind a bush, its spiky branches brushing against her bare arms. She didn't dare peek out in case Deirdre was searching already.

She heard giggles and whoops as some of the others were caught. She stayed where she was, waiting.

She heard footsteps getting close and held her breath. Could she dodge around the bush and escape? But then Deirdre pounced on her. Game over!

When it started to get dark, it was time to head home. Sonia and her friends strolled back together, not wanting the evening to end. As they came to Catherine's road, Lisa got a wicked look in her eye.

'I dare you to knock on the door and run away!' Lisa said.

'OK. But you're doing the next one!' Catherine replied.

The other girls huddled in a bunch behind the hedge, watching as Catherine crept up to the front door, hoping not to be seen. They laughed at her terrified expression as she rushed back to them.

'You should see your face!' Lisa choked.

'Let's see you do it then!' Catherine said.

One by one, the girls took turns to tiptoe up to a front door, press the bell, then run and hide, giggling to themselves as the irritated homeowner came out to peer down the road.

'Now you, Sonia!' Eileen said.

Sonia hesitated. The house they had just come to had the longest driveway on the road. And there were no trees or bushes to hide behind – just wide, smooth lawns on either side.

Lisa saw her hesitation. 'No bother to you, girl!' she said. 'You're the fastest of any of us!'

'Go on then,' said Sonia, never one to refuse a dare.

She was almost holding her breath as she crept up the driveway, watching the windows for any sign of movement. She stood poised on the doorstep, hand outstretched to press the doorbell, body already pre-pared to run.

Ringgggg!

Sonia turned and fled, her footsteps light as she dashed down the driveway, diving behind the hedge to the safety of the group of girls. Her heart raced with the thrill of running, the thrill of not being caught.

'Look!' whispered Lisa, peeping around the hedge.

Sonia peeped too. There was a whole line of cross-looking mammies standing on their doorsteps.

'Those kids!' one said to her neighbour.

'Have they nothing better to be doing?' she replied.

The girls pressed their hands over their mouths to stifle their giggles.

When Sonia got in, there was a lovely surprise waiting. Dad was home!

'Dad! Why are you back already?' Not waiting for an answer, she ran into his arms for a big bear hug.

'Whoah, don't knock me over,' Dad protested, but he was beaming from ear to ear as he held her tight. 'My ship got in early! So you lot will have to put up with me for a few extra days this time.'

Dad was in the Irish Navy and was often away from home for weeks at a time. Sonia loved when his ship was docked at Haulbowline and he would take herself, Gillian and Tony on board for a look around.

Mam was pottering about making tea, in that contented way she did when she had all the family around her. 'Good timing,' she said. 'You'll be able to take Sonia to the Milk Run on Saturday!'

'I'm looking forward to it already!' Dad said.

CHAPTER TWO

THE COBH MILK RUN

he Milk Run was always a special event in Cobh. It seemed to Sonia that everyone in the town was taking part. If they weren't running in the race themselves, they were going to help out as stewards, or giving out the prizes, or just coming to watch and cheer on everyone taking part.

The Milk Run went all around the island of Cobh. It was quite an adventure to go to the other side of the island, especially on foot and with all your friends for company. Sonia always enjoyed the day out. There was a great atmosphere around Cobh, with the streets hung with bunting and everyone stopping to chat to each other as they made their way to the race.

Sonia had been busy getting people to sponsor her to take part in the race. She'd gone around to neighbours' houses and they'd each filled in a line on her sponsorship card, agreeing to donate something for each mile she completed. The Milk Run was ten miles long! With lots of people taking part they could raise plenty of money for charity.

At the halfway point in the race all the runners got a chance to have a bit of a rest and a glass of milk straight from the big churns in the farmer's field. Then they'd be full of energy for the rest of the race!

Sonia got to the halfway point and gulped down her glass of milk while she waited for her friends. Christine caught up with her first.

'I thought I could keep up with you, but you were too fast for me!' she panted.

Sonia laughed. 'I was just dying for a drink, so I sprinted that last bit!'

Johanna joined them next. 'Quick, get me some milk, I'm dying here!'

The girls sat down on the grass with their milk, enjoying watching all the runners coming into the field looking badly in need of a break. Some of the faster ones had already taken off again and were well on their way to finishing. But the Milk Run wasn't really a race – it was all about the fun of taking part together, not about who finished first.

Feeling refreshed after their break, the girls got to their feet once more.

Sonia was jogging along, feeling a bit full after her glass of milk, when a man who was also running in the race caught up with her. Running alongside her, he said, 'You know, you'd probably be pretty good at cross-country running.'

Sonia pictured the island of Ireland on the big map hanging up in her classroom. Surely he couldn't mean running the whole way across the country?

'What is that?' she asked cautiously.

The man laughed. 'It just means running through the countryside – country lanes, fields, mud, all that, you know? Not on a road like this one.'

'Oh, OK,' Sonia said.

The man moved on. Sonia watched him go, thinking about what he'd said. She liked the idea – the sounds and smells of the countryside all around her. And the feel of soft grass under her feet, instead of the hard tarmac surface of roads. She'd give it a go some time, she decided.

Sonia and her friends thought it would be fun to join Ballymore Cobh Athletics Club. They'd heard all about the fun that club members had, getting to travel to represent the club at races all over Cork and beyond. Then there were the end of term discos which were legendary!

Being part of a club would give the girls a chance to learn more about running technique and improve their fitness and stamina. Sonia was excited about getting to develop her running properly.

Sonia was glad to have her friends with her when she went to her first training session. It might have been a bit awkward not knowing anyone. But she soon realised they were kept far too busy to have a chance to feel shy or uncomfortable.

First they did a warm-up jog. Then the coaches got them to do a faster run, and then put them through a series of sprints.

Sonia was exhausted by the time the session ended! But she was also on a high. It was brilliant to find a tribe of people who enjoyed running as much as she did.

'Well done, Sonia,' the coach told her at the end. 'You've got great potential – keep it up!'

Sonia glowed.

CHAPTER THREE

COMMUNITY GAMES

'**A**ll right class, it's time for PE! Line up there please, nice and quiet now.'

PE was Sonia's favourite subject. She sometimes found it hard having to sit at a desk all day. It was especially tough on sunny days, when she'd find herself staring out the classroom window, longing to be out under the blue sky running around with her friends. PE always broke the day up nicely.

Miss Byrne waited until the boys and girls had formed a neat line.

'Now, we're going to be doing some running today, and practising the high jump and long jump. Can anybody tell me why?'

'Are we training for the Olympics?' asked John,

who always had something cheeky to say.

The class tittered, but Miss Byrne remained serious. 'Close, John! We're training for the Community Games.'

A series of 'ooohs' went through the group.

Sonia loved taking part in the Community Games. It was a big competition for children with lots of track and field events – races and relays, high jumps and long jumps, shot put and javelin throwing. When you weren't busy taking part yourself, you could hang around with your friends watching other people's events, and there was a tuck shop where you could buy treats.

Miss Byrne led the class outside and told them to jog slowly around the playground to warm up. Some of the class started complaining they were tired after just one lap, but Sonia was dying to start running properly.

Miss Byrne lined them up in groups. They were going to run 100-metre sprints first. Sonia wasn't so keen on sprints, but she did her best and came second.

Next was 400 metres – twice around the yard.

'Urgh, that's too long,' Deirdre complained. 'I'm

tired already.'

Sonia bounced from one foot to the other. 'Just don't start off too fast,' she advised her friend. 'That's what most people do, then they have to stop!'

Sure enough, John, Mike and Elaine took off at the same pace as they'd run the 100 metres. Sonia held back, and Deirdre, puffing a bit anyway, stayed with her. Before they'd finished the first lap, John and Elaine had both slowed down to a walk and Mike, although he was still running, looked shattered.

'Come on, we can catch up with Mike now!' Deirdre said.

Sonia knew instinctively that it was still too soon. 'Not yet,' she said. 'Keep going at this pace. After we pass Miss Byrne we'll make our move.'

'OK,' Deirdre agreed.

They passed John and Elaine, who tried to speed up again but couldn't.

'Now!' Sonia said just as they got to where Miss Byrne was standing, watching them all with a critical eye.

Sonia sped up and Deirdre did her best to keep up with her. Mike realised how close they were behind him and tried to go faster, but he was exhausted. He could only watch as the two girls passed him out.

'Last stretch!' Sonia said. 'Final spurt, OK?'

'You go on,' Deirdre panted. 'I can't go any faster!'

Sonia hesitated. She didn't want to leave her friend. Then she realised Clare and Gerard were coming up behind them. They'd gone for the slow and steady approach too and still looked like they had plenty of energy left.

Sonia wasn't going to be beaten by those two! She spurted, a streak of green in the brown play-ground, reaching Miss Byrne a good ten metres ahead of the next pair.

'Well done, Sonia!' Miss Byrne said. 'You're going to do us proud at the Community Games!'

Over the next few weeks Miss Byrne gave the chil-dren lots of chances to practise their running. They did it every week in PE, and some of the children stayed on after school to do some more training.

All the hard work paid off. At the Cobh Com-munity Games, Sonia won the 800-metre race! This meant she could go on to represent Cobh at the bigger event in Cork city.

Lisa came running up to give her a hug. 'Well done, Sonia! And guess what – I won the 200 metres! So we'll get to go on the bus together!'

'That's brilliant!' Sonia said, hugging her back. Days out were so much more fun when you had a friend to share it with.

Mam was delighted to hear Sonia's news.

'Isn't that great?' she said. 'Sure aren't you always running everywhere? Now you have a medal to show for it! And another day out to look forward to!'

'You'll be the best of the lot of them,' Dad declared. 'You'll be running for Cork next!'

'Can I go too?' Gillian, Sonia's little sister, wanted to know. 'I can run very fast!'

Sonia laughed. 'Maybe when you're older,' she told her. She felt very proud to be representing her town at the Community Games.

The day of the games was bright and sunny. Sonia

felt so excited as she got on the mini-bus with the other children from Cobh. She had her packed lunch in her bag – sandwiches, an apple and a packet of crisps. More importantly, she had money to buy a few treats!

'Here you go, love, buy yourself something nice,' Dad had said as he waved her off, pressing some money into her hand.

They had a sing-song on the bus to pass the time. They got so loud that the bus driver shouted at them to keep it down. Sonia and Lisa giggled to themselves, hiding behind the seat in front of them.

'We're here!' shouted Mike.

Sonia and Lisa pressed their faces to the bus window. The Community Games were being held at a community centre with a running track outside. A huge banner hung across the entrance, welcoming all the participants. There were people milling around everywhere, excited children messing about, pushing and shoving each other, while parents and coaches tried to keep them under control. A couple of adults with clipboards and baseball caps seemed to be in charge.

Sonia thought back to the first time she had taken

part in the Community Games. She was very small, only about seven, and so excited to be running in her first race. She had done the sprint with a big gang of seven-year-olds. She didn't even remember who had won, but she did remember the nun, Sister Rosario, who had a big box of lollipops waiting for them at the end, win or lose.

Now it suddenly felt much more serious. She was running for more than a lollipop – she was running to represent Cobh, and maybe even win!

The bus pulled up in the car park, and the children tumbled out. Sonia and Lisa went to check when their races were on. They had a little while to wait, so they found a good spot near the finish line where they could watch the other races.

'I wish our races were on first!' Sonia said.

'I know!' said Lisa. 'Then we could just relax and watch the rest. Now I'm all nervous!'

They cheered loudly for some children they knew. John came second in his race, so that was a pretty good result for Cobh.

When it was time for Sonia's race, she found her nerves had disappeared. She just wanted to run!

She was thrilled when she crossed the finish

line in first place. She'd beaten girls from all over County Cork! It was a fantastic feeling to win her first big race.

CHAPTER FOUR

BORN TO RUN

Summer was nearly over. Soon it would be time to start secondary school, and all the changes that would bring. The holidays had gone far too fast, just like they always did!

That day, Sonia and her friends had spent the afternoon hanging out at the sea front. Now she and Deirdre were strolling home together.

'Come on,' Deirdre said. 'Let's see which way home is faster.'

'OK,' Sonia agreed, immediately feeling a little thrill of excitement. She already knew which way would be faster. It would be whichever way she went!

'I'll go this way, down by Mrs O'Brien's house,'

Deirdre decided. 'And you go around by Mrs Dennehy's, OK?'

Sonia thought about it, picturing the two routes in her mind. Going past Mrs O'Brien's was the most level route. Mrs Dennehy's house was on a hill, and it meant having to cross a couple of roads, maybe having to wait for traffic to pass by. She thought it was probably longer, and it was definitely trickier. But she was still confident she could be quicker than Deirdre.

'OK,' Sonia said again. 'Do you want to say go, or will I?'

'I will,' Deirdre declared, getting into a starting position, leaning forward a little with her arms bent at the elbows.

Sonia smiled to herself, copying her friend's pose.

'Ready?' Deirdre asked.

'Ready,' said Sonia.

Deirdre tried to build up the tension. 'On your marks. Get set. GO!!!'

They both took off, Deirdre at top speed, building up a quick lead. Sonia wasn't worried. She knew Deirdre couldn't keep up that speed for very long.

Sonia turned the corner, losing sight of her

friend. She was running steadily – she knew she could run faster, but there was a long way to go and she needed to save some energy.

She dodged past a woman pushing a pram, and narrowly avoided a dog who ran into her path, barking.

'Bet you can't keep up with me,' she told him, laughing.

As she approached the first crossroads, Sonia watched for traffic. There was a car about to pass the point where she needed to cross. Nothing was coming in the other direction. Once the road was clear, Sonia sped up – she needed to take her chance or she'd lose time. She was right on track.

Now came the hill. It was steeper than Sonia had pictured it. She hadn't had time to recover from her spurt across the road, and she felt her lungs were bursting as she raced up the hill. She was glad to get to the top and enjoyed the easy run down the other side.

Sonia was coming to the last stretch of the run. She pictured where Deirdre would be. Would she be leaning against the wall at Mrs O'Brien's house, clutching her side where she'd got a stitch? Or would she have got her second wind by now and be charging down towards the finish line?

Sonia turned the corner. Home was in sight, just at the end of this row of houses. There was no sign of Deirdre. Sonia was tired now, but she was determined to keep her pace up, just in case Deirdre suddenly appeared.

She'd made it! Sonia leaned against the pillar to get her breath back. The thrill of the win surged through her.

By the time Deirdre turned up, panting and red-faced, Sonia was sitting on the wall swinging her legs.

'Looks like your way was shorter then,' Deirdre said, before collapsing in a tired heap on the ground.

'That must be it,' Sonia said with a smile.

Later that week, Sonia and Mam went into town to buy everything she needed for starting at Cobh Vocational School. As well as her uniform, she'd got a new schoolbag big enough for all her books, and tons of new stationery.

They came home laden down with bags.

'Why don't you show Dad your new uniform, Sonia?' Mam said.

'Oh, yes!' Sonia ran off down the hall to her room.

She quickly changed into her new uniform, admiring it in the mirror for a moment before she sauntered down to the kitchen, dying to show Dad.

'Well now, don't you look smart!' Dad said. 'My goodness, is that really my little Sonia?'

Sonia grinned. She felt very grown up in her new uniform. Already primary school seemed like a long time ago.

CHAPTER FIVE

SECONDARY SCHOOL

Starting second level at Cobh Vocational School meant a big change. Sonia now had a longer school day and lots of new subjects to study like French and business studies. But what she was most excited about was the chance to play on school teams like camogie and basketball, and especially to represent the school at athletics.

Sonia loved to run. She would run to and from school, her hair flying out behind her, her schoolbag bouncing on her back.

Tony's school was up the hill from hers, so if she got out a minute early at lunchtime she could just about get past his school before they were out. If not she'd have more kids to dodge past as she dashed home! Past the tennis club, past the GAA club, past the swimming pool – then it was a straight run home.

She set herself little goals. She'd make it to that traffic light before the red car. She'd run from that lamp post to the postbox faster than she had yesterday. She'd run right up that hill without slowing down.

Nothing could beat that feeling of freedom, her feet barely seeming to touch the ground, the exhilaration of seeing how fast she could go.

After lunch, Sonia would leave it as late as possible before heading back to school. Then she'd run at top speed to catch up with her friends outside Kelleher's sweet shop before they strolled back the rest of the way together.

Sometimes, out alone after school, she did homework in her head while she ran, reciting French verbs, or Irish poems, or trying to remember the new theorems she'd learned in maths.

She was in a world of her own as she ran along the streets of Cobh.

In the camogie team for Cobh Vocational School, Sonia was always put in midfield because she was a fast runner. Midfielders did the most running, needing to help out in defence and also get the ball up front to the forwards. Today they were playing a school from Cork city, one of their big rivals.

Sonia stood shivering as she waited for the game to start. Soon it was underway and she was running here, there and everywhere, trying to get in a good position for her teammates to pass to.

She won the ball, and straight away heard Linda shouting. 'Pass, Sonia!'

Sonia whacked the sliotar as hard as she could. It wasn't a great pass, but Linda managed to catch it and sprinted downfield. Sonia watched as she sent the ball neatly over the bar. She wished she could be as coordinated as Linda was.

The game was underway again. Emer passed the ball to Sonia, who tried to head downfield with it. But the big full forward from Cork crashed into her, sending her flying. She lay on the ground for a moment, struggling to get her breath. Camogie could be so rough sometimes!

'Come on, Sonia!' shouted Aoife.

Sonia got to her feet. Emer had won the ball back and passed it to Aoife. But now the Cork girl had it again and was heading right for her.

'Tackle!' shouted the coach.

But Sonia held back. She didn't want to get injured. She had a cross country race coming up! She half-heartedly stretched out her hurley, but the Cork girl easily passed her by.

Cobh lost the match by four points. The coach wasn't happy. 'We should have won that match, girls,' she told them. 'We need to fight harder next time!'

Sonia was just glad it was over. She set off to cool down on a slow jog home, loving the freedom of being able to just run, out on her own and with no one crashing into her.

Later, standing in the shower with the water running over her aching muscles, it hit Sonia that she didn't want to play camogie any more. It just wasn't for her. She hated the stop-start running. She felt uncoordinated with a hurley in her hand. She didn't like being constrained by the rules. And she was constantly afraid of getting injured. What if she had really hurt her ankle today? She wouldn't have been able to take part in the race with the club on Sunday.

That was it, Sonia decided. From now on she was going to stick to running.

CHAPTER SIX

THE ATHLETICS CLUB

The best bit about being part of a club was all the trips. Sonia loved piling into someone's car with a gang of her friends, singing songs and giggling all the way there.

'Pipe down back there!' Dad would say when it was his turn to drive. 'I can hardly hear myself think!'

But he'd grin at Sonia and she would know he didn't really mind.

Even better was when they hired a minibus so they could all travel together. Then the sing-songs were legendary!

Their favourite place to go was Youghal because they sometimes got to go to Perks Funfair on the way home. That was the perfect treat after a race! And the Friday evening meets in Midleton and Carrigtwohill, on grass tracks, were always a good way to end the week.

There was a cross country race on Sunday that they'd all been gearing up for. Every morning when she woke up Sonia checked the weather. Would it ever stop raining? The course was going to be a sea of mud.

On Sunday morning, the skies were still grey but at least it wasn't raining.

Mam packed a flask of hot tea for Sonia to take with her. 'You'll be glad of it after your race!' she said. 'Best of luck, Sonia!'

The girls were excited to be heading off on the bus together.

'It's going to be a muddy one, girls,' Pat, their coach, told them. 'But sure you're well used to that! You're in great form and I reckon we'll be coming home with a trophy today.'

At the cross country team events, every runner had a part to play in helping their team to win. Each person's finishing position counted towards the team's score, so they all had to try to pass as many runners as they could. Ballymore Cobh were winning a lot of prizes at the moment, and Sonia loved that feeling of being part of a winning team.

As usual, they'd got there early, which meant shivering in the field while they waited until the last possible minute to take off their tracksuits.

'We must be mad,' Catherine grumbled. 'We could be at home right now watching TV!'

Catherine was always grumpy before a race, especially when it was cold. But afterwards she'd be hopping around the place with excitement.

'Just think of crossing that finish line,' Deirdre told her.

'Someone better have a cup of tea for me afterwards, that's all I can say!' Catherine said.

'You can have some of my tea – but only if you run well!' Sonia teased her.

'All right girls, time to get changed,' Pat told them.

There was more grumbling as the girls took off their tracksuits, stuffing them into their kit bags. They stood waiting in their shorts and Ballymore Cobh singlets, rubbing their arms to try to warm themselves up.

Sonia pulled on her spikes, the special running shoes for running cross country, made to cope with the rough terrain. She hoped it wouldn't be much longer until they got going!

At last they were off. This course took them across fields, up and down slopes. The ground was bumpy and uneven and there were patches of mud everywhere. Tree roots crossed their path, and they needed to be on the lookout for obstacles that could trip them up.

Lisa sank into a boggy bit of ground almost up to her knee! She had to yank hard to pull her foot free.

Soon the girls were splashed from head to toe with mud, and breathless from tackling the rise and fall. Cross country running was so much tougher than running on a track or road! But Sonia loved the freedom of being out in the countryside.

She looked over her shoulder to see how her team-mates were doing. The familiar black and yellow of Ballymore Cobh was easy to spot. The girls were all holding their own, though some looked more drained than others by the tough conditions.

Just when Sonia thought the finish line would never appear, she came over the top of a hill and saw it in sight, with supporters waiting to cheer them on. Sonia summoned up the last bit of energy she had for one final spurt. She was thrilled to cross the line in first place.

Sonia bent over double, leaning her hands on her knees as she tried to get her breath back. That had been a tough one! She raised her head to watch her teammates cross the line one by one. It was looking good!

Sonia went to find her flask of tea, sharing with Catherine as she had promised. She had never been so glad of a hot drink!

When the results were announced, Sonia was thrilled to hear that Ballymore Cobh were in first place! The girls squealed in delight, throwing their arms around each other, not caring any more about the mud and the wind and the cold.

On the way home, they pestered Pat to let them stop at Mandy's chipper.

'Ah go on, go on, go on …'

'Pleeeeeeeease!'

'You're athletes!' Pat said, like he did every time. 'You should be eating healthy food!'

'We'll have fish burgers,' Sonia told him. They

were all convinced that fish burgers were the food of champions.

It was the best feeling coming home from the race, the club trophy carried proudly at the front of the bus, and then stopping at Mandy's. Eating chips out of the bag and licking their salty fingers, they chatted and laughed about all that had happened that day, and what they'd do next.

CHAPTER SEVEN

A NEW COACH

Sonia kept hearing people talking about a brilliant coach called Sean Kennedy. He took kids for training sessions on the hills up behind the reservoir. He was obsessed by the science of running, and had read dozens of books on the subject. He was a big fan of Peter Coe, who had coached his son, Sebastian Coe, from when he was very young right up to the Olympics. Sean had looked at every session Sebastian had ever done! He came up with his own versions, adapted for the people he coached.

'You should ask him to train you, Sonia,' Pat said. 'He knows more about middle distance running than I do.'

Sonia went home and told her mother what Pat had said.

'Sure give him a ring, why don't you?' Mam said. 'You've got nothing to lose!'

Sonia looked up his phone number in the big yellow phone book beside the phone in the hall. She dialled the number, twirling the phone cable around her finger as she waited for him to answer.

Sean agreed at once to help Sonia out. 'What I'll do is, I'll write out a few weeks' worth of training routines for you,' he said. 'I'll give them to you when I see you, or if I don't I'll put them in your letterbox on my way to work.'

'That's brilliant,' Sonia said. 'Thanks a million!'

Sean laughed. 'No need to thank me, just get out there and stick to the plans, that's all I ask!'

'Oh, I will,' Sonia said.

Sean was as good as his word. He put the first training schedule in the letterbox the very next day. Sonia studied it carefully. She reckoned she could manage this easily.

That day after school, she rushed through her homework and headed out to a field. Sean had said to work on 100- and 200-metre sprints. Trouble was, she wasn't sure how far that was. She looked down the field. That tree would do as a marker for 100 metres, she decided. And the end of the field was probably about 200 metres. Close enough, anyway! She set off.

At the end of the session, Sonia was tired but happy. She felt so good when she was running – like she could do anything.

As soon as she got home, Sonia filled in the first entry in her training log. She looked at the rows of white squares and imagined them all filling up with her running records. It was brilliant to have a proper plan in place to help her be a better runner.

The weeks went by, and Sonia stuck to the schedule. No matter what else was going on, she never missed a run. After school she ran around the green beside Cobh Vocational School, enjoying the freedom of the wide open space and the fresh air before she had to settle down to homework. Other days she ran up Birds Hill, a steep slope a kilometre long, or up the Burma Steps, a series of steps that stretched for 800 metres.

She became a familiar sight to the people of Cobh, always running, always pushing herself.

As she ran she often found herself playing the commentary to an Olympic final in her head. 'And it's O'Sullivan coming up on the outside … O'Sullivan of Ireland in the green is passing out her rivals … she pulls ahead … no one can catch her now! Gold medal for Sonia O'Sullivan!'

She could almost see the cameras flashing and hear the roar of the crowd as she ran around the empty field.

Sean was great at encouraging Sonia. He'd sit down with her at the kitchen table to go through the training plan. She was always pushing him to make it harder.

One day, he met her after she'd finished a session, and asked her why she was so shattered.

'Did I give you too much to do today?' he wondered. 'I didn't think the session was too hard.'

'It wasn't hard enough,' Sonia told him. 'So I did

it uphill!'

Sean laughed heartily. 'You're something else, Sonia. You're going to be the best runner in Cork before we know it.'

'I don't just want to be the best in Cork,' Sonia suddenly burst out. 'I want to be the best in the world!'

There. She'd said it, the words that had been building up inside her for months. She waited nervously, hoping Sean wouldn't laugh.

But Sean was completely in earnest. 'Sonia, there's no reason why you can't be,' he told her. 'And I don't say that to everyone, believe me. You have the natural ability, so all you need to add to that is hard work. And I know you're willing to do that. Some of these sessions I've given you – other athletes have just given up. They tell me it's too hard. You don't – you just come back looking for more. So keep it up – you put in the miles and the results will come!'

That night, when Sonia went to bed, her dreams seemed a little bit closer.

CHAPTER EIGHT

UNDER THE WEATHER

All day at school, Sonia had felt miserable. She was cold and shivery, and her nose wouldn't stop running.

Now she stood outside her back door, examining her reflection in the window. Her eyes were a bit watery, and her nose definitely looked swollen and red from being wiped with a tissue all day. It was a damp, drizzly evening in Cobh, and she knew that if her mam and dad realised she was sick, there was no way she'd be allowed to go out running later. She practised putting on a big smile and a bright voice.

She put her key in the door. 'I'm home,' she called, dumping her bag in the corner of the kitchen and throwing her wet coat over a chair.

Mam was making dinner, while Gillian sat at the kitchen table doing her homework, and Tony played on the floor.

'How was school?' Mam asked as she stirred the saucepan.

'Yeah, it was grand,' Sonia said. 'I got loads of homework though.'

'Poor you!' said Mam. 'Help yourself to a snack there.'

Sonia put on some toast and busied herself getting out a plate, butter and jam, careful not to stand too close to Mam in case she noticed her red nose and eyes.

'Mam, how do you spell conscience?' Gillian asked.

'Sonia will help you there,' Mam said. 'I can't leave this saucepan just now.'

Sonia was glad to have an excuse to go over to the table. She spelled out c-o-n-s-c-i-e-n-c-e for Gillian, waiting while she carefully printed it out in her copy.

The toast popped, and Sonia quickly spread it with butter and jam. 'I'm off to my room,' she said.

'I'll get started on my homework because I need to fit in a run later.'

'OK love,' Mam said.

Phew! Looked like she had got away with it. She'd have her toast, Sonia decided, and get her maths homework done, then she'd head out for a run before dinner. She'd go before Dad got home and the chance of being caught increased!

'I'm off,' Sonia called as she headed for the door.

She was glad she'd got out for a run, but she felt even worse as she plodded along the street. Her legs felt like lead and every breath was an effort. Her head throbbed. But she was determined to keep going. She just couldn't miss a run! Not now when she was training for the Munster Schools under-14 race.

The rain was only getting worse and it took Sonia ages to warm up. By the time she got home she felt warm from the run, but she still couldn't stop shivering.

'Dinner in five minutes, Sonia!' Mam said.

'OK,' Sonia said, dashing down the hall to the bathroom. She'd just have time to hop in the shower. She didn't want to sit down for dinner in her wet running gear.

Standing under the hot running water, Sonia tried to imagine it warming up her aching bones. She breathed in the steam, thinking it might help clear her lungs. But that just set her off coughing.

Mam was dishing out the dinner when Sonia came back to the kitchen, wearing her favourite blue pyjamas and with her hair wrapped up in a towel. Normally Sonia was starving after a run, but she had no appetite today and just pushed the food around on her plate.

'Are you feeling all right, Sonia?' Mam asked. 'You're not eating.'

'I'm grand,' Sonia said quickly. She crammed some potatoes into her mouth.

'Are you sure? Your nose is a bit red,' Mam said, looking closely at Sonia.

'It's just a bit cold out today, that's all,' Sonia said, her mouth full.

'Hmm,' said Mam. 'I hope you're not coming down with something.'

Sonia said nothing. She was glad when Tony started telling Mam about his football match, and seized her chance to escape to her room.

She lay on her bed for a minute, trying to summon up the energy to go back to her homework. Her eyes wandered to all the Liverpool posters she had covering her walls. She wondered how her favourite players coped when they were having a rough day.

Sonia struggled through the rest of her homework, then went down to watch a bit of TV with Mam. Gillian and Tony were already in bed. It was nice being the oldest and getting to stay up a bit later! But tonight Sonia couldn't stop yawning.

'I think you'd better get an early night, young lady!' Mam said. 'You nearly swallowed me with that last yawn!'

Sonia wasn't going to argue. 'I'm a bit tired all right,' she admitted. 'Night so, Mam.'

'Night, love. And if you're a bit under the weather in the morning you're to take it easy, do you hear me? No trying to run with a cold!'

'I'll be grand,' Sonia said.

She shuffled off to bed, glad she was already in her pyjamas. She just about had enough energy to brush her teeth.

In bed, she couldn't stop coughing. She buried

her face in the pillow, trying to drown out the sound. She didn't want Mam hearing and deciding she was too sick to run!

By the time race day came around, Sonia was feeling much better. In fact, she felt ready to take on the world!

She checked her spikes, which she'd carefully washed in the sink after her last run. She always took good care of them – they were her most important piece of gear.

She had her shorts and singlet ready and her race number. She was good to go!

It was a tough race, with some really good opponents – the very best of the thirteen-year-olds from all over Munster. Sonia felt strong and powerful as she raced along the cross country route, cheered on by supporters from her club and her family.

Crossing the line in first place was an amazing feeling. Sonia felt rewarded for all the hard work she'd put in, those days when she felt tired or sick, but went running anyway. Mam and Dad came running up to give her a hug, as proud as punch.

Next day her picture was in the local paper.

'Well, will you look at that?' Dad said, a huge smile on his face. 'My little girl, in the paper if you don't mind!'

It made Sonia happy to see how proud they all were of her. Her only complaint was that there was no all-Ireland race for the under 14s! She felt like she'd have a chance to win that too!

'Plenty of time for that,' Dad said with a laugh. 'Just enjoy the moment, pet!'

CHAPTER NINE

A TRIP TO DUBLIN

Sonia was so excited to be heading to Dublin for an athletics meet at Santry Stadium. Mam made sure she was up in plenty of time and that she had a good breakfast before she headed off.

'Now, you have your money for your ticket?' she asked.

'Yep,' said Sonia.

'And your spikes?'

'In my bag.'

'And you haven't forgotten clean underwear?'

'Mam!' Sonia was blushing. 'I've got everything, OK?'

'All right so,' Mam said, kissing her on top of her head. 'Have a great time!'

Dad gave Sonia a lift to the train station.

'Best of luck!' he said as he dropped her off. 'Run like the wind!'

Sonia was meeting up with girls she knew from other running clubs around Cork.

'Sonia! Over here!'

Michelle and Mairead were waving frantically to her. Sonia ran to join them in the ticket queue.

'We've got a plan,' Michelle told her, a wicked grin on her face. 'We're just going to buy three tickets between the whole lot of us. We can spend the rest on sweets!'

'But won't the inspector come around and check our tickets?' Sonia asked.

'It's grand,' Mairead said. 'Some of us can hide in the toilets!'

Sonia grinned. 'OK so!'

Breda, Stephanie and Tara came to join them, and Michelle filled them in on the plan.

Mrs Murphy, Michelle's mam, was travelling with the girls to look after them. She came to check that everything was all right before she headed off to her own carriage with her book.

'My head would be wrecked listening to you lot

all the way to Dublin!' she declared.

The girls were delighted to be trusted to travel on their own. It was their first big trip away.

They sang songs for the first little while, then started sharing out their snacks. They were taking it in turns to look out for the ticket inspector.

'Who's going to hide in the toilets?' Mairead asked, as Michelle took over her watch.

'I will,' Breda said at once.

'Me too,' said Sonia.

'No, you need to stay and talk to the inspector,' Mairead said. 'You've got the most innocent face, he'll believe you!'

Sonia protested, but the others all agreed that Mairead was right.

'He's coming!' hissed Michelle.

The four girls all fled for the toilet, where they squashed into the tiny cubicle together, trying not to giggle.

Sonia did her best to look nonchalant. Michelle casually strolled back to her seat. Sonia couldn't look at her in case she burst out laughing.

The two girls waited, holding their breath, until the inspector got to them.

'Tickets?' he said.

Sonia held out the three tickets. The inspector glanced from her to Michelle.

'The other girl is in the loo,' Sonia said, giving him her sweetest smile.

The inspector just grunted. He stamped their tickets, handed them back and moved on.

Sonia and Michelle exchanged grins. So far so good!

'I hope they don't come out too soon!' Michelle whispered.

'They won't!' Sonia whispered back.

All the same, it was a tense wait until the inspector had moved on to the next carriage. Sonia slipped out to the corridor and knocked on the toilet door three times – the signal that the coast was clear. Mairead, Breda, Stephanie and Tara took it in turns to nonchalantly wander back to their seats.

The Cork girls had a great day out at the Santry Sports, collecting a whole host of medals. Sonia looked at her medals with pride as they headed back to the hotel where they'd be staying the night. They'd look good with the rest of her collection!

Mrs Murphy took them all to McDonalds to celebrate with burgers and milkshakes. While the others were finishing their food, Michelle and Tara sneaked out to the shop next door, returning with bulging pockets and knowing grins.

'Did you get the sweets?' Sonia whispered.

'Yep – and something else too!' Michelle told her. 'I'll show you back at the hotel!'

They were staying in adjoining rooms. Mrs Murphy went for a cup of tea in the hotel bar, leaving the girls to get ready for bed. As soon as she was safely out of the way, Michelle and Tara showed the other girls what they had bought.

'Water balloons!' Sonia exclaimed, tearing open a packet. 'Brilliant!'

Mairead ran to the en suite to fill one at the sink. Too impatient to wait, Sonia filled hers from the bath tap.

'Wait! We have to divide them up!' Michelle said. 'We'll take these to our room, OK? Room 212 versus Room 211! Go!'

She and Tara went tearing off to fill their balloons

in their own room, with Breda running after them.

'Come on!' Sonia said to her roommates. 'They'll be trying to sneak back in here, but we can hide behind that trolley outside.'

Trying not to giggle, the three girls squeezed in behind the trolley which the hotel staff had left in the corridor, filled with mini shampoos and clean towels. They didn't have long to wait before Michelle, Tara and Breda appeared.

'Gotcha!' cried Sonia, throwing her balloon which burst and soaked Michelle from head to foot.

Mairead's balloon hit the wall above Tara's head, splashing her hair, while Stephanie's fell at her feet, soaking her furry slippers.

'AAAAAAAH!' shrieked the girls.

Sonia and the others made a dash for the safety of their room. Tara tried to throw her water balloon after them, but it just hit the door as it slammed behind them.

'We'll get you!' Tara vowed.

Sonia, Mairead and Stephanie collapsed on the floor in a giggling heap.

CHAPTER TEN:

NATIONAL CROSS COUNTRY CHAMPIONSHIP

As she started going to races regularly, Sonia would see the same faces there again and again. There was a girl called Diane McCarthy who ran for a club called Grange Fermoy. She was a brilliant runner, and Sonia was frustrated that, one race after another, Diane would beat her.

Then out of the blue, Sonia's day came, and she finished ahead of Diane.

'Don't get cocky about it now,' Dad warned. 'There'll be someone else coming along who'll beat you.'

Dad was right. The next person Sonia came up

against was Anita Philpott. Anita ran for North Cork, a club who had a top-class coach and always won lots of medals.

The competition between the two girls was fierce. Anita's coach was Fr Liam Kelleher. He also happened to be the editor of *Marathon,* the running magazine which was read by runners all over Ireland. Every time a new edition came out, the girls would be checking to see whether he had included more photos of Sonia or of Anita!

At the Munster Championship in Thurles, everyone was talking about whether Sonia or Anita would come out on top. There was great excitement about watching these two talented girls grow and develop as runners. Which of them would win?

In the end, it was neither. Out of nowhere, another girl, Carmel McCarthy, streaked past them both to claim the prize. Sonia was gutted.

'Run your own race next time,' Dad advised. 'You can't control what any other runner does, the only person you're in charge of is yourself.'

Finally, at a schools meet on a windy day, Sonia beat Anita. It was only by a fraction of a second, but the gold medal was hers. Sonia was thrilled to have

beaten her long-time rival at last. But she didn't rest
on her laurels – she just moved on to the next goal.

Watching athletics on television was always exciting. Sonia would picture herself lining up at the
startline with all the other athletes. She thought she
knew just how they felt – stomach full of butterflies, wanting to get going, hoping all the training
would prove to be enough.

Sonia was glued to the 1984 Olympics. Her running hero, Marcus O'Sullivan, was taking part in
the 800 metres and the 1500 metres. Sonia had everything crossed for him – it would be just brilliant
to see a Cork athlete succeeding on the Olympic
stage. Unfortunately it wasn't to be Marcus's day.
Sonia had been following his career closely and she
knew he was better suited to running indoors. Sure
enough, at the 1985 European Athletics Indoor
Championship Marcus won a silver medal in the
1500 metres. Sonia was delighted to see him on
the podium. She dreamed of the day when she too
might win a medal for Ireland.

★ ★ ★

Sonia was starting to aim higher and higher. In February 1987, she won the National Junior Cross Country Championship. On a high after the race, she told Sean that she wanted to enter the senior championship which was coming up in just two weeks.

'I'm not sure about that, Sonia,' Sean said. 'It's a big leap from junior to senior.'

Sonia knew Sean was only thinking of what was best for her. She was still only seventeen after all. But the thought of running in a senior race where she'd be competing against some of the best athletes in Ireland was so exciting. She knew too that Anita Philpott was planning to run it, and she thought that if Anita could do it then so could she!

'I'll go for it,' she decided.

She went off and entered herself in the race, confident that she could give it her best shot.

She had heard that an athlete called Caroline Mullen was the favourite for the race. She was a talented runner who was on a scholarship at an American university. She had won a bronze medal in the US collegiate championships, and she was coming home to Ireland especially for this race.

The race was being held in Killenaule in County Tipperary. Sonia's dad paid the late entry fee for her.

She was amazed to see Sean and his wife Mary there, with their baby in the pram.

'What are you doing here?' she asked him.

'Ah sure, I couldn't miss it,' Sean told her. 'If you're going to win this thing I want to be here to see it!'

Sonia was touched to see his faith in her. There was an extra bounce in her step as she made her way to the start line.

It was a tough race over muddy fields, up and down hills and over uneven surfaces. But Sonia was in her element. She loved the feel of the grass under her spikes as she ate up the miles.

When the leaders began to break away from the rest of the pack, Sonia was in fourth place. The reigning champion, Mary Donohoe, was in the lead, closely followed by Caroline Mullen, and then Ann Buckley. Sonia knew she was in star-studded company, but she believed she had what it took to succeed.

On the final lap, Caroline made her move. Sonia

went with her, running steadily just behind her, waiting for the right moment to overtake her.

With 300 metres to go, Sonia accelerated, passing Caroline out in one smooth swift motion. As she closed in on the end she felt sure she had the race won. Her whole face was lit up with joy as she crossed the finish line.

Sonia found herself surrounded by cameras. Journalists were crowding around to ask her questions, which she did her best to answer.

'What now?' one of them asked.

Sonia blurted out her most heartfelt wish. 'I'd like to run in the Olympics, but sure I'll take each day as it comes.'

Later, Sonia wondered if she'd said too much. Would people think she was full of herself, thinking she was good enough to run in the Olympics? Should she have just laughed off the question, said that her next goal was to celebrate with a fish burger and chips?

But deep down, she knew she had to be true to herself, and that she had taken the first tentative step on a road that would take her all the way to that Olympic dream.

CHAPTER ELEVEN

VILLANOVA

The Leaving Cert mock exams were tough going. Sonia's teachers kept reminding the students that it was just a practice run for the real thing, but it was hard not to feel under pressure.

Sonia found that running was a great way to relieve the stress. All her worries felt far away as she was pounding the pavements of Cobh. And instead of feeling tired after a run, she felt energised and ready to get stuck into her work.

The other kids in Sonia's year were starting to talk about what they wanted to do when they left school.

'I want to be a vet,' Sinead said. 'I just love the thought of being able to work with animals all day.

The points are so high though!'

'I'm going to do arts,' John said. 'I'm not really sure what I want to work as yet so at least it won't pin me down too much!'

'I wouldn't mind doing that too,' said Orla. 'Or maybe languages.'

Aoife made a face. 'I've had enough of sitting at a desk all day. I'm just going to get a job. It'll be great to have my own money at last!'

Accountancy was Sonia's favourite subject and she was very good at it, so her teachers were encouraging her to apply for business courses. But what Sonia was really hoping for was to become a professional athlete.

Sonia had read all about other Irish athletes who had gone to American universities on a scholarship, like Caroline Mullen who she had beaten in the National Cross Country Championship. She knew that was the next step for her if she wanted to make progress in her running career.

Being offered a scholarship would mean that all her university fees would be paid. She could study accountancy while also being trained in athletics by some top coaches. In return, she would represent the university in races.

The University of Arizona and Providence College were both interested in Sonia. But it was Villanova, a small university in Philadelphia, that Sonia was most attracted to.

Villanova wanted to fly Sonia over to see the university and find out what they had to offer. She'd go over during the Easter holidays so she wouldn't have to miss school. Sonia couldn't quite believe it. While the other kids from Cobh Vocational School were chilling out, enjoying lie-ins and the break from the school routine, or getting stuck in to revising for the Leaving Cert, Sonia would be strolling round the campus of a famous university on the other side of the Atlantic.

Two girls from Villanova, Cassie and Colleen, met Sonia at JFK Airport in New York.

'So, you want to head straight for the green fields of Philadelphia, or should we see a bit of the city first?' Cassie asked, a twinkle of mischief in her eye.

'I'd love to see the city,' Sonia said straight away.

It was her first time in New York and she definitely didn't want to waste the opportunity!

'We thought you might say that,' Colleen grinned.

Sonia's eyes were wide as she took in all the sights of New York on the drive in to Manhattan from the airport. She couldn't believe she was really there! They drove up Fifth Avenue, down Broadway and through Times Square. Cassie took a wrong turn and they had to make a U-turn, the three girls just giggling wildly as the New York City drivers blasted their horns at them.

Cassie found a parking spot to let Sonia step out of the car and gaze up at the skyscrapers towering above them, taking in the noise and bustle and the enticing smells of food from dozens of different cuisines.

'When you're in New York, you gotta have pizza,' Cassie declared.

So they found a pizzeria and crammed into a booth together. Sonia's mouth was watering at the sight of the pizza oozing cheese and tomato sauce.

'Try the hot peppers,' Colleen suggested.

Sonia hadn't had them before, but she sprinkled them all over her pizza like salt.

'Whoah, go easy!' Cassie said.

Sonia took a huge bite and nearly choked at the fiery taste, but she just grinned and said, 'Yum!' She wasn't going to admit that it felt like her whole mouth was on fire!

When they got to the Villanova campus the girls had another surprise in store for Sonia.

'Guess what,' Cassie said. 'Look who's here to show you around the campus!'

The Irish athlete Marcus O'Sullivan stood in the Philadelphia sunshine, waiting to meet his namesake.

Sonia was completely starstruck. She couldn't believe she was meeting her hero. She had just watched Marcus winning the World Indoor Championship, and now here he was.

'Welcome to Villanova,' he told her.

'Hey, you two aren't related, are you?' Colleen joked.

'Not as far as I know!' Marcus said.

'Maybe everyone in Cork is called O'Sullivan!'

Cassie laughed. 'Why don't we leave you two Irish-ers to it? See ya later, Sonia!'

Sonia got over her shyness as Marcus showed her around. She was soon asking him question after question about his time there, which he answered freely. Sonia realised Villanova was going to be the perfect fit for her.

CHAPTER TWELVE

AMERICAN ADVENTURE

Six months later, Sonia stepped off the plane in JFK once more, ready to begin her American adventure. But there was one small issue – she was on crutches, her right leg in a cast.

'It's just a stress fracture,' the doctor had reassured her. 'A few weeks' rest and you'll be as right as rain.'

The coaches made her take the cast off, insisting she didn't need it. Sonia found it all very stressful, but she was keen to make a good impression.

While she was recovering from her injury, Sonia spent a lot of time in the pool. She did pool running, wearing a floatation belt called an aqua jogger. This was much gentler on her body than running, and it helped her to strengthen her muscles and to keep her fitness up.

But she kept getting injured again. It was so frustrating! Sonia felt that running on roads and hard tracks was causing the injuries. Her American coach, Marty Stern, didn't agree. He kept pushing her to try harder, and Sonia kept getting injured.

It wasn't easy combining an accounting degree with training as an athlete. Sonia had a very full schedule, needing to fit in all her classes and coursework as well as her training sessions. She started every day with a run, then had a shower and breakfast before heading off to her classes. At lunchtime she would have a training session with her teammates, then another shower before getting stuck into the rest of her college work.

After spending so many years training on her own, Sonia loved having other girls to train with. They pushed each other on, sometimes competing, sometimes encouraging each other. If you were having a bad day, there was always someone there to pick you up.

At weekends the athletics team often travelled to track and cross country races where they would represent Villanova as a team. Sonia would have to pack not just her running gear but her textbooks too, so she could study on the bus or in between warm-ups and races.

The athletes were under a lot of pressure. Not only were they expected to go out and win medals for the college, they also needed to keep up with their academic work. When they missed classes due to an athletics meet, they were expected to get the notes and catch up.

It was full on, but Sonia had always thrived on being busy. She knew how lucky she was to be able to go to college on a scholarship and to get professional coaching in the sport she loved. She had four years to develop and grow as an athlete, in an environment that nurtured her talent and gave her opportunities to improve her skills in races. It was just so hard to deal with the injuries. Sometimes it felt like she was taking one step forward and two steps back.

Two years into her course at Villanova, Sonia felt it wasn't going well at all. She had arrived in America full of potential as a runner, and now she was going nowhere. She sometimes felt like giving up and going home to Cobh to get a job.

It was a relief to get home for the summer holidays. Sonia got a job in a pub which meant working evenings. She'd get up late every day, go for a six-mile run and then lie around the house for the rest of the day.

Sonia was glad to catch up with her old coach, Sean Kennedy.

'How's it going in Villanova?' he wanted to know.

'Not great,' Sonia admitted. 'I keep getting injured.'

'Ah, that's not good. Why are you getting injured?'

'I think it's running on hard surfaces,' Sonia said. 'It's the impact, you know?'

'So go back to running on grass,' Sean said.

It was such simple advice – but it was the wake-up call Sonia needed. She knew what had worked for her in the past; she just needed to do it again.

Sean told Sonia all about fartleks. The funny name made her laugh, but the concept was just what she needed. Fartlek was a Swedish word meaning 'speed play', and it was a way of mixing up training with different speeds, running at top speed as far as a random target (maybe a tree or a pole) and then doing an easy jog to recover. It helped with both speed and endurance, and it made training more fun.

It reminded Sonia of when she was a teenager running home from school, and she'd run as fast as she could to beat a car to a lamppost, then slow down to get her breath back before taking off again.

Back at Villanova, Sonia started doing fartlek sessions on the grass, and once more found that Sean's advice was spot on.

January came around, and all Sonia's teammates were planning on doing their sessions inside, working on the indoor track.

'Why don't you come and train inside with us today?' Caro suggested.

It was so tempting to join them. Sonia thought of the numbness in her fingers from running outdoors, the bite of the wind on her cheeks, the burning sensation in her lungs from breathing in cold air. But she shook her head. She knew her own body and what worked best for her. 'No, thanks. I need to be outside.'

'Oh, come on, it's freezing out!' Kate said. 'Save the outdoor running for spring!'

'Thanks, guys, but I'll catch you later!' Sonia said, lacing up her runners.

She ran through white fields, snow and ice crunching under her feet with every step. When she got towards the end of a session, tired and wanting to stop, she would picture herself winning a race against her opponents, and she would keep going.

During her years at Villanova, Sonia helped the athletic team to win all sorts of prizes. She also ran in the World Student Games in Sheffield, winning gold in the 1500 metres and silver in the 3000 metres.

Villanova was the perfect introduction to the world of the professional athlete. Sonia knew now what it was like to race against the best athletes in the United States and across the world. She had built up lots of race experience which had helped her develop the skills needed to win when tactics were just as important as speed.

She was coming towards the end of her degree

course, and it was time to start planning for life after college. Growing up, Sonia had had no idea that you could make a career out of running. In the races she had won as a teenager the prizes had been things like tracksuits, and, once, a projector that she had sold for £100.

But at the highest level, there was funding available to support the best athletes. There were races with big prize money, and sponsorship to be had. With Sonia's talent and experience, she could make a living out of doing what had started off as a favourite hobby.

She talked it over with Mam on the phone.

'Not long to go now,' Mam said. 'Will you come home to Cobh when you're finished over there in the States? There's plenty of work to be had here in the accountancy line!'

Mam knew full well that despite her new degree accountancy was the last thing on Sonia's mind.

Dad was on the other phone so they could all chat together. 'Our girl is going to be far too busy winning medals to worry about a real job!' he said proudly.

Sonia laughed. 'I hope you're right, Dad!' she said.

'I'm going to give it my best shot anyway. I don't think I'll be coming back to Cobh, but I'll be a bit closer to home anyway. I'm going to move to London – it's a good place to train. I need to get myself a coach!'

London proved to be the perfect fit for Sonia. And being a full-time athlete was fantastic. After all the years of juggling studying and training at Villanova, it was brilliant to be able to concentrate on what she loved most. She would go out running twice a day – the track in the morning, and the gym or the park in the afternoon. She began working with a coach called Kim McDonald who had a great reputation for helping athletes achieve their full potential. He would create the right training plans for her just as Sean Kennedy had once done.

Kim was her agent too, which meant that she didn't have to worry about the logistical side of things. There was so much more to being a professional athlete than Sonia had realised. It wasn't all about the high-profile competitions like the

Olympics or the World Championships. There was a whole circuit of races year round, and she needed an agent to organise it all for her, decide which races she should enter and make all the travel plans. There were sponsorship deals to be done and contacts to make. It was great to have Kim looking after all the organisation so she could focus on running.

Sonia knew the athletics world was starting to take her seriously. She had won some great races. But for her they were just steps along the way to her big goal – the 1992 Olympics in Barcelona.

CHAPTER THIRTEEN

BARCELONA

Sonia walked to the start line with the other athletes, her tummy full of butterflies. She could feel the eyes of the crowd upon them. Sixty-five thousand people, all there to watch their race.

She glanced up and saw the Olympic flame, burning bright orange against the dark Spanish sky. A jolt of excitement ran through her. This was the Olympics! She had dreamt about this moment for so long, and now it was here.

Sonia looked at the other athletes around her. She had raced against many of them before. She knew they had fought hard to be here in the final of the 3000 metres.

There was her friend, Alison Wyeth from England. The American athlete, Patti Sue Plumer, always seemed to have bad luck – a year earlier, just before the World Championships, she had been bitten by a dog! Yelena Romanova and Tetyana Dorovskikh used to run under the flag of the USSR, but since that country had broken up they were now running for the Unified Team.

Then there was Yvonne Murray from Scotland, who Sonia saw as the favourite for the race. She had won a bronze medal at the last Olympic Games in Seoul. Sonia wondered what it must be like to have that medal tucked away in your locker.

And here among them all was Sonia, a girl from Cobh in County Cork, twenty-two years of age and competing in the Olympic Games for the very first time. She knew she deserved to be there as much as any of them. She was longing for this chance to show what she could do.

Sonia thought back to the first race she could remember – the Community Games back home in Cobh. Lollipops were waiting when you crossed the finish line. Sonia remembered the delight of putting her hand into the big box to pull out a lollipop. But more than that, she remembered the thrill of racing and winning.

Sonia hopped from one foot to the other, feeling impatient. She wished the race would start. Standing and waiting was the worst part! She wanted to be on the move, running around this great stadium, flying past the crowd and the lights and the noise.

Looking into the enormous crowd, Sonia suddenly caught sight of a familiar face. It was her dad, smiling down at her, love and encouragement clear in his face. Sonia's heart lifted as she smiled back at him. She couldn't believe that out of all these thousands of people she had spotted her dad.

He was too far away for Sonia to be able to hear what he was saying, but Sonia thought she knew. 'Just enjoy it, kid!' he'd be saying. 'It might be the Olympic Games, but it's still only a race.'

At last they were calling out the athletes' names. When she heard her name, Sonia stepped forward and gave a little wave. On the screen she could see a giant version of herself do the same thing. Millions of people around the world were sitting at home watching that same image on TV. Sonia tried not to think about that. She needed to stay focused.

The runners got into position. The starting gun

fired. They were off!

At first the pace seemed a bit slow. Sonia had expected some of the runners to take off really fast, but she knew she had to pace herself. She had been in races before where someone set off too quickly and couldn't keep that speed up. They led all the way only to be beaten at the end.

Sonia was determined not to let that happen. She would wait for the right moment and then make her move.

Alison Wyeth took the lead. Sonia stayed where she was in the middle of the pack. It was too early, and the runners were still keeping up a steady pace. Sonia kept running, trying to keep her nerves under control, always watching out for someone to break away.

They were coming towards the last lap. As the group came down the back straight, Yvonne Murray moved to the front.

'This is it!' Sonia thought. 'I need to go with her. I can't let her get too far ahead.'

Picking up speed, Sonia moved to the front of the group and took up her position just behind Yvonne. Now maybe they could open up a gap to the rest of the group.

But Yvonne didn't keep up the pace, and the other runners were right behind Sonia, breathing down her neck. All of a sudden, Sonia realised that Yvonne was exhausted. She had sprinted too soon, and all her energy was gone.

She dropped back, leaving Sonia alone at the front of the group.

Sonia panicked. What on earth should she do now? She hadn't expected to be out in front so soon. There were still 300 metres to go, and she knew she couldn't keep her top speed up for that distance. And the other athletes were hot on her heels.

Sonia gritted her teeth. She would just have to run as hard and as fast as she could. Maybe sheer determination would get her through!

The crowd were roaring, wanting the pace to pick up, hoping someone would make a move. Flashes from cameras lit up the stadium. Thousands of faces, flashing lights, flags and banners – everything was a blur as Sonia kicked on. She couldn't see the other competitors, but she could hear their footsteps thundering just behind her. She hadn't managed to shake them off.

They reached the last bend.

'Come on!' Sonia told herself fiercely. 'Just another hundred metres to go! Hang in there!'

She could see the finish line. In her mind's eye, she could see herself crossing it in first place, climbing on the podium, getting the gold medal.

But Sonia was out of fuel. She had given everything she had.

Yelena Romanova flew past on her right, just a dark blur.

'Keep going, keep going!' Sonia told herself desperately. 'I can still get silver!'

But a split second later Tetyana Dorovskikh passed her on the left.

Sonia ran as fast as she could, arms pumping, pushing hard. Desperately willing herself to keep going, Sonia could only watch as Angela Chalmers of Canada passed her on the right. Three athletes in front of her, and only three medals to be won. The chance was gone.

Sonia crossed the finish line in fourth place and collapsed on the ground, out of breath and absolutely devastated. Fourth – the loneliest spot on the leaderboard. Just 0.19 seconds behind the third-place finisher. She couldn't believe she had come so close to an Olympic medal, and yet so far.

As she watched the three medallists celebrate their victory, Sonia promised herself that she would be back. Next time, Sonia vowed, she would run harder than ever, and she wouldn't make any mistakes. Next time, she would be on that podium.

CHAPTER FOURTEEN

SONIA GOES TO STUTTGART

The year 1993 marked a fresh start for Sonia. The World Championships were taking place in Stuttgart in Germany, and she knew she had a real chance for a medal. She was being talked about as the favourite for both the 3000- and 1500-metre races.

After Barcelona, Sonia had become a household name in Ireland. Sports fans all over the country had felt deep sympathy for her after her fourth-place finish. Now they were eager to see what she was going to do next.

Throughout the spring, Sonia won race after race. At the Bislett Games in Oslo, she set a new personal best for 3000 metres, in a time of 8:28.74.

It was a time that was twelve seconds faster than Romanova's gold medal winning time in the Barcelona Olympics. The world of athletics was talking about Sonia and her great potential.

There were rumours starting to spread that a Chinese athlete had run an even faster time, but it was easy to dismiss this as just gossip. It wasn't shown on TV, so there was no proof it had happened at all.

All the same, it was surprising to hear so much talk about the Chinese athletes. China wasn't known for having a record of producing great athletes. Their breakthrough on the international scene seemed to have come very suddenly.

Sonia was feeling confident when she got to Stuttgart. She was having a good season and was sure she was going to peak at just the right time.

It was exciting to be in this German city which had a special place in the hearts of Irish sports fans. When the Republic of Ireland soccer team had played in their first ever European Championships, Stuttgart was where Ray Houghton had scored his famous goal in their victory against England.

As all the athletes arrived at their hotels and training grounds, more rumours were spreading about the Chinese athletes.

'They say they've got a new diet,' another athlete told Sonia. 'They drink turtle blood! It's supposed to be an amazing source of energy.'

Sonia pulled a face. Drinking turtle blood? Revolting! But she was curious to see these athletes who had got everyone talking about them.

At the warm-up track, the Chinese athletes appeared dressed identically. They did the exact same warm-up and ran together for the whole session. The other athletes were fascinated at how they seemed to move perfectly in unison. Sonia started to feel a little worried, but the heats were coming up. Heats were like semi-finals which the athletes competed in to see who would qualify for the final. She'd soon find out how good these athletes really were.

A few nights before the heats, Sonia woke from a nightmare. She had dreamt that when she arrived at the stadium, her heat had already started! She had to run flat out to try to catch up with the other athletes, knowing she'd never be able to make it in time to qualify for the final. It was a dream that felt far too real, and left Sonia feeling very shaken.

When the real heat came around, Sonia did her best to put her worries to one side. She knew what she had to do to qualify. The first four from each heat would go through, as well as the three fastest losers from all heats.

Sonia found it relatively easy to win her heat. She didn't run at her top pace, needing to save something for the final, but still finished well ahead. This was a good boost to her confidence. But watching some of the other heats, it was a little worrying to watch familiar opponents like Yvonne Murray and Yelena Romanova being easily beaten by Chinese athletes.

Sonia got talking to some of the athletes she knew ahead of the final.

'What do you think the Chinese girls are going to do?' she asked.

'I think they'll go flat out from the start,' Alison Wyeth replied. 'Try to scare everyone off.'

'I think so too,' Yvonne Murray said. 'I've heard they don't have a final kick.'

The 3000-metre final was scheduled for Monday evening. It was a warm, humid evening in Stuttgart.

Sonia arrived at the stadium feeling nervous but determined. This was her moment, she told herself. This was the night when she would find herself on the podium.

The first 1000 metres felt very slow to Sonia. She was watching the three Chinese girls – Qu Junxia, Zhang Linli and Zhang Liron – to see what they would do. The speculation had been wrong – they didn't take up the lead and push from the start. She was surprised to see the time of 2:59.06 on the board for the first kilometre – that was slower than she had expected.

But the pace soon increased dramatically. Yvonne Murray made a little burst, but Sonia remembered what had happened in Barcelona. She kept up with her, but she didn't panic – it was too early for a serious move.

It was a little intimidating the way the three Chinese girls seemed to be running as a team. They talked to each other throughout the race, making space for each other when they needed to. From the stand, their coach, Ma Junren, was shouting instructions. They took it in turns to lead, and kept on changing the pace, confusing the other athletes and disrupting their rhythm.

As the race went on, the athletes got more spaced out. The three Chinese girls were out in front, with Yvonne close behind, and Sonia just after her. Sonia bided her time, confident that when they started to pull away she would be able to go with them.

There was about 700 metres left to run when Sonia realised Alison was right at her shoulder. She hadn't known she was so close behind her, and it unnerved her.

In that moment's distraction, the Chinese girls pulled away. All of a sudden they were gone. Sonia panicked. Had they spurted too soon? Should she go with them now, or call their bluff? Was it better to save something for a final kick?

She made up her mind to go, but her hesitation was to be fatal. A gap was already opening up between Zhang Lirong in third and Yvonne in fourth. An even bigger gap lay between Yvonne and Sonia.

Gritting her teeth, Sonia stepped up the pace. She passed Yvonne, who looked shattered. Now she was in fourth place, but the three Chinese girls, still running in close formation, were well ahead.

The bell sounded for the final lap. Already Sonia knew that she wasn't going to win this race. The girl in third place, Zhang Lirong, was ten metres ahead of her. Sonia concentrated on reeling her in. She could still finish among the medals.

But it wasn't to be. There just wasn't enough track left to make up the gap. Sonia could only watch as, one after the other, the three Chinese athletes crossed the finish line ahead of her. Fourth place again, that most heart-breaking of positions. So close, and yet so far.

Bitterly disappointed, Sonia checked the finish times. Her own time of 8:33.38 was more than four seconds slower than the winner, Qu Junxia. But what was even more devastating was the knowledge that it was even further behind her own Irish record which she had set just five weeks earlier in Oslo.

She hadn't lost because she wasn't fast enough. She had lost because she'd got her tactics wrong. It was a cruel blow.

Running home from the stadium that evening with her coach Kim, Sonia decided she would deal with the disappointment in the same way as she had dealt with every other defeat. She would learn something from it, and come back fighting.

CHAPTER FIFTEEN

A SECOND CHANCE

There was still the 1500-metre final to go. Sonia was determined to approach it in a different way. She wouldn't let the Chinese girls dominate the race by running together as a team – she would just make sure she got in there and broke up their little group. Even if she could just beat one of them, that would be enough.

By now the whole athletics community was talking about the Chinese athletes. They had dominated the women's track events, from 1500 metres right through to 10,000 metres. In fact people were even saying that the 10,000-metre champion Wang Junxia would have been capable of winning all those events herself, as well as the marathon, if the schedule had allowed.

Rumours were going around that their times couldn't possibly have been achieved cleanly. They had come out of nowhere and beaten established athletes. People were saying that it was impossible to improve that quickly without cheating by using performance-enhancing drugs.

Sonia tried not to listen to the rumours. There was nothing she could do about it anyway. All she could do was to concentrate on her own training, her own record. She knew she had the talent to be up there with the best.

The 1500 metres wasn't Sonia's favourite distance. It was all over so quickly, there wasn't much time to use all the skills she had learned about race tactics. But after the disaster of the 3000 metres, it was her only chance to come home from the World Championships with a medal.

The race was about to start. Looking around the stadium, Sonia saw that a medal presentation ceremony was just starting. It hit her that after last year's Olympic Games and the 3000-metre final last week she had missed out on two major chances for a medal. She couldn't let another chance pass her by.

Sonia glanced around at the other athletes. There was a different group of Chinese girls in this race, but they all had the same coach, Ma Junren. Liu Dong was the World Junior champion over 1500 metres. Lu Yi was also a junior champion at 800 metres, and Yan Wei made up their team. Sonia was determined not to let them run together as the girls in the 3000 metres had done.

Angela Chalmers from Canada was another one to watch. Then there was Hassiba Boulmerka from Algeria, the reigning World and Olympic champion. Sonia knew she had overcome many obstacles to have such a successful athletic career, coming from a Muslim country where attitudes to female athletes were still very conservative.

They were off! The athletes watched each other closely as the race got underway, with most of the attention focused on the Chinese girls – three white vests. Once more Ma Junren, their coach, was shouting instructions from the stand. His voice was very distinctive, and the athletes and the crowd knew exactly where he was. Some spectators started jumping up and down in front of him, waving flags, making noise – anything to stop his instructions getting through to the runners as they went past. It seemed that whatever their nationality, supporters didn't want to see the Chinese athletes walk away with all the medals once more.

Four hundred metres to go. Liu Dong took off. The tension levels went through the roof. Close behind was Lu Yi, then Hassiba Boulmerka, with Sonia once again in fourth place. This time, she didn't panic. She knew she had more in the tank.

Two hundred metres to go. Sonia accelerated. Seeing the screen at the far end of the stadium, she realised Liu Dong had too big a lead on her – but she was convinced she could beat the other two. She passed Boulmerka. She passed Lu Yi. She was racing as hard as she could and the finish line was in sight.

Silver! She had done it! She'd finished in second place, and the silver medal was hers. Boulmerka came up behind her to finish in third, and Lu Yi was left in that old familiar place that Sonia knew too well – fourth.

The stadium went wild. All the tension that had built up exploded into a cacophony of screams and cheers and whoops.

Liu Dong, the gold medallist, went on a lap of honour and the crowd went silent. It was clear that she wasn't a popular winner. Then Sonia and Hassiba Boulmerka went on their laps of honour, and suddenly the crowd was on its feet again. Sonia was over the moon. Of course she would have loved to be the outright winner, but to come second in the world – the whole world! – was a pretty amazing feeling.

CHAPTER SIXTEEN

A GOOD YEAR

The next year, 1994, was a good one for Sonia. She began ticking off records, one after another. In July she set a new world record in the 2000 metres in Edinburgh. Just a week later, she broke the 3000-metre European record in a time of 8:21.64. A year earlier, this would have been a world record, but the arrival of the Chinese athletes on the scene had changed all that. The four fastest times in the world were all Chinese. Sonia was fifth.

She ran the fastest time of any athlete that year in the 1500 metres, the mile and the 3000 metres, and the second fastest in the 5000 metres. She set four new Irish records. Everyone was talking about this talented runner from Ireland who was dominating middle distance running.

Everything was building up to the European Championships in Helsinki. Fans had bought their tickets and made travel plans, and the city was buzzing with preparations for this big event.

Journalists and fans alike were wondering what events Sonia would decide to enter.

Sonia made up her mind to just run in the 3000 metres. She had had a good season over that distance – except for the last three races. People were starting to say she had done too many races that season and was worn out. People said she wouldn't find it easy.

Sonia felt sure she could prove them all wrong.

There was a carnival atmosphere in Helsinki, with sports fans from all over Europe gathering to cheer on their heroes.

Sonia tried to shut out all the noise and excitement and stay focused on her race build-up. When race day came around at last, she spent most of the day in bed, resting her legs and preparing herself mentally for the race.

The stadium was packed full. Sonia looked out for Irish flags in the crowd. It always gave her a lift to see supporters from home. It would be a big day for Ireland if she could win this race. Sonia was hoping to be the first Irish woman to win a medal at the European Championship.

Without the Chinese athletes, Sonia's main rival was Yvonne Murray once again. At the last European Championship, Yvonne had won the gold medal and Sonia had finished eleventh. Quite a gap to bridge! But this year Sonia had won the last three races between them. Maybe her time had come.

There was another familiar face in the race too, and she was also in the green of Ireland. Anita Philpott, Sonia's old rival in their teenage races in Cork, had qualified too. The Irish fans were cheering them both on, though they knew Sonia had the best chance of a medal.

The race followed a familiar pattern – Yvonne setting the pace, Sonia close behind. With three laps to go, the pair had opened up a gap of thirty metres to the rest of the girls. Over the next lap they doubled that distance.

Sonia was feeling strong. She wasn't going to let Yvonne win this one.

With 200 metres to go, Sonia pulled away.

Yvonne battled on, but Sonia was too fast for her. She crossed the line in 8:31.84. She had won! Her first major championship victory.

Yvonne hung on for second place, followed by a strong third-place finish by Gabriela Szabo, a Romanian girl who had won the world junior title just a few weeks earlier.

Sonia was elated. All that hard work had been worthwhile. She had got this one right, and now she would have the medal to prove it.

At the medal ceremony that followed, Sonia felt ready to burst with pride when she saw the Irish flag being raised over the stadium, the highest of the three medallists' flags. When the old familiar strains of Amhrán na bhFiann were played, it was truly a special moment. She heard the Irish fans singing along, knowing her name would go down in the record books. She was the first Irish woman to win a European Championship athletics medal.

The next few years seemed to stretch out in front of her full of glittering possibilities. The World Championships in 1995. The Olympics in 1996. Sonia was at the peak of her career, and gold medals were hers for the taking.

CHAPTER SEVENTEEN

GOING FOR GOLD

Back in London, Sonia fell into her normal routine. Her day started at 8am, when she'd get out of bed, pull on her runners and go for an easy twenty-minute jog. She felt like she wasn't properly awake until she'd had a run. Then she'd head home for breakfast of toast and coffee and get ready to start her day.

After breakfast it was time to head to the track. Even though it wasn't part of her running schedule, Sonia had a habit of timing how long the run to the track took her. Her normal time was 23 minutes and 13 seconds – sometimes longer if someone got in her way, like a little old lady or a dog!

Sonia enjoyed meeting other athletes at the track.

It was good to know they were all in it together. She chatted to them while doing her stretches and warming up.

Then it was time to get down to hard work. Some days she would start with a 2000-metre run, then work down through 1000, 800, 400 and 200 – each run getting faster. Other days she would focus on the 5000 metres, which meant a longer session. It was great to work with a pacesetter over this distance. That year there were a lot of Kenyan athletes living and training in London, and they were a great help with this.

After her session, Sonia headed home for an ice bath. Sometimes the last thing she felt like doing was getting into that freezing cold water, but she had been told it was the best way for her muscles to recover. Sometimes too she'd go for a massage to ease any aches and pains.

The rest of the afternoon was time off. Sonia enjoyed reading, or meeting up with other athletes for coffee, or chatting to her family on the phone. It could be lonely being away from home, so it was always good to catch up with them. And it definitely helped that Teddington was like a small

Olympic village with so many other athletes living nearby.

Around 5pm Sonia would go for another run. She often met up with a bunch of runners at Bushy Park where they'd go for a gentle evening jog. Her namesake Marcus O'Sullivan was one of the group, along with Frank O'Mara and Paul Donovan. They'd talk and laugh as they jogged along, catching up on news from home or chatting about the latest film releases.

Bushy Park was a huge, flat park, home to a herd of deer, with a maze of tracks and pathways. It was perfect for running, and very popular with both professional athletes and casual runners.

It was strange when they passed ordinary people out for a run. Sonia could tell someone was running their very hardest, red-faced and out of breath, yet Sonia and her group could pass them out easily, still chatting away and feeling very comfortable in their stride. It made her realise how lucky she was to have a body that was built for running and to be able to do what she loved as a career.

Another World Championship beckoned in 1995, this time in Gothenburg in Sweden. Sonia was in top form and felt sure this would be her year.

The women's 5000 metres had been added to the schedule for the first time. It was a distance Sonia enjoyed, and felt confident in.

The day of the race arrived at last. Sonia had a race-day routine that she always stuck to. Her running gear lay ready on a chair, her runners lined up underneath. She ate loads of bananas, her favourite pre-race food, and drank gallons of water so she wouldn't feel dehydrated later. She went for a light run to loosen up her legs.

She spent the afternoon watching the men's marathon on TV, wishing the time away.

At last it was time to go to the stadium. At the warm-up track, Sonia went through her usual routine of stretches, high steps and short warm-up runs. She watched the other athletes out of the corner of her eye, knowing they would be doing the same to her.

There was Fernanda Ribeiro, who Sonia had run against several times that year already. Gabriela Szabo, who'd finished third at the 3000 metres in

Helsinki. British athlete Paula Radcliffe was showing signs of promise but hadn't yet found the event
that suited her best. The Kenyan runners, Sally and
Florence Barsosio and Rose Cheruiyot. The small
Swedish girl, Sara Wedlund, who was so fair that she
reminded Sonia of the Milky Bar kid from the TV
ad, and Sonia's old friend, Gina Procaccio.

The three Chinese athletes who had claimed the
three medals at the 3000 metres two years earlier
were not competing. They had disappeared from
the international scene as suddenly as they had
arrived.

Forty minutes to go. Sonia slipped into a porta-
cabin to change into her Irish vest and shorts. It
was always a great feeling putting on those green
colours, knowing she was representing her country.

Thirty minutes to go. Sonia gathered up her
things and concentrated on getting focused for the
race ahead.

The last call sign flashed overhead. Kim pinned
Sonia's number on her top and reminded her of
everything they had planned. She knew what she
needed to do.

Along with the other athletes, Sonia made her

way to the holding room, where they would wait until they were called out on to the track. Everyone was given a basket with their number on where they could leave their belongings. The air was thick with tension. Some people avoided eye contact, keeping busy with their belongings or just staring at the ground. Others strode about confidently as if they hadn't a care in the world.

The athletes were called out. Sonia was first out – as usual she was dying for the race to begin. She lined up on the track behind the white line. Fernanda Ribeiro was right beside her. Poised and ready, they waited.

Crack! The pistol sounded and the race began. Gabriela Szabo set the pace early on. Sara Wedlund made occasional bursts. Paula Radcliffe took the lead when she felt the pace was getting too slow. But it was Fernanda who Sonia was most conscious of as they raced round and round the track.

The finish was getting closer and closer. A thousand metres to go – 800 – 600 … Sonia began to feel more confident. Now all that mattered was who would make the first move, and when. She had the strongest final kick, so if Fernanda left it too late, Sonia knew she could beat her.

There were just three of them out in front now – Sonia, Fernanda, and a Moroccan girl, Zahra Ouaziz. Gabriela and Paula were further back.

They were approaching the bell for the final lap when Fernanda sped up. Sonia stayed with her, never letting her get more than a metre ahead.

With 250 metres to go, Sonia prepared to make her move. She moved outside Fernanda, ready to overtake her. Straightaway she realised that Fernanda had no comeback. This race was Sonia's to win.

Now there were only 200 metres to go, and Sonia was running harder than ever. She felt invincible as she focused on that line, absolutely determined to reach it first.

She crossed the line. Sonia was World Champion – the first ever female 5000-metre champion. She was on top of the world!

Fernanda finished in second and Zahra third. Zahra rushed to hug Sonia, thrilled with her medal. They waved to the crowd together.

Her dad was right behind the advertising hoardings, waiting for her. She ran to him and gave him a big hug. He held her close, telling her how proud he was.

Now for the lap of honour. Sonia didn't really enjoy this part – she felt awkward and embarrassed, she didn't know what to do with her hands. But the loyal fans in the stadium were screaming her name, and she knew she owed it to them.

Someone handed her an Irish flag. It was on a huge, heavy pole. Sonia lifted the flag, delighted at all the cheers that greeted her. But the pole felt so heavy in her tired arms. She knew she wouldn't be able to carry it all the way around the track. She put it down and set off, little knowing that there would be a negative reaction.

Finishing her lap of honour, Sonia posed for photos, and one of the Irish photographers gave her a small flag, which she proudly held up. But at the press conference that followed, the journalists seemed very bothered about the fact that she had put down the first flag.

Sonia couldn't believe this was all they were talking about. She was a world champion for the first time ever! Ireland's first female world champion!

Next she had to do a television interview with

John Treacy, the Irish Olympic medallist who was now working for RTÉ.

'Here, Sonia, put this hat on,' he suggested, handing her an Ireland baseball cap.

Sonia looked at him in shock.

'Damage limitation,' John explained.

'Are you serious?' Sonia said. 'I can't believe you want me to wear a hat to show how much I love my country!'

John tried to reassure her, but Sonia was struggling not to look upset.

'It's OK Sonia, you can get through this,' John promised.

They did the interview with Sonia holding the hat instead of wearing it. She was glad to get it out of the way.

It was the only dark cloud on what had been a truly amazing day, one that Sonia knew she would remember for the rest of her life.

CHAPTER EIGHTEEN

ATLANTA

Being Sonia, she didn't take time to just enjoy the feeling of being World Champion. She was already looking to her next goal. Next year was an Olympic year – always the most important in any athlete's calendar. The Games would be held in Atlanta, and Sonia was looking forward to having another chance at an Olympic medal. She remembered the awful disappointment of finishing fourth in Barcelona, and felt sure she could do better this time.

So after Gothenburg it was straight into another series of races and training. She went straight to Zurich and ran a 3000-metre race, then to Cologne for a mile race, then back to London for more training. Then it was right back on a plane to Brussels for a 5000-metre race, which she ran despite feeling hot and unwell.

The next few months were a whirlwind of long plane journeys and one race after another. Sonia was wearing herself out, feeling worse and worse on each run. But she refused to acknowledge how she was feeling. With the Olympics getting so close she didn't want to show any sign of weakness. She didn't realise she was running on empty – and that sooner or later she would have to pay the price.

The Olympics were the peak for every athlete. There was just something so special about them. The excitement that built up all around the world, among the media and the athletes and the ordinary members of the public, gave it an extra edge over every other competition. Winning a World Championship medal was an amazing achievement. But to have an Olympic medal – to go down in history as an Olympic champion – that was what every athlete strove for.

Sonia thought of Ronnie Delany. He had won his place in Irish history with his Olympic victory in Melbourne in 1956. All these years later, he was still a national hero. Those old enough to remember the race could tell you exactly where they had watched it. Those who were too young had heard all about it from parents or grandparents and knew what a special moment it was.

Then there was Eamonn Coghlan, who was one of Ireland's most successful athletes when Sonia was growing up. He won the 5000-metre race at the World Championships in 1983 – Sonia remembered watching his ecstatic celebrations. He was one of the finest indoor runners in history. But he had finished fourth in two Olympic Games, and now he would never have an Olympic medal.

Sonia dreamed of seeing her name in the record books. Of being a champion that the whole of Ireland would be proud of. Running in the fields of Cobh as a child, or on the tracks at Villanova as a student, it was the commentary to an Olympic final she had playing in her head.

The Olympics came every four years, meaning each athlete had only a few chances in their career of winning that most precious of medals. Sonia had seen the chance pass her by in Barcelona. She didn't know what would happen between now and the

Sydney Olympics in 2000. She could only focus on Atlanta 1996, and all her energies were devoted to it.

She ignored any signs that she was feeling a bit run down. All the aches and pains, the times she had to stop a training session, the days when she felt completely lacking in energy. Even when she was running well she didn't feel good, but she just pushed those feelings away and kept her eyes on the prize of the Olympics.

She and Kim were arguing about her training sessions. She was doing press conferences and interviews and photo shoots. It was one thing after another, and she was feeling more and more stressed, but she just kept going.

Traditionally athletes had always stayed in the Olympic village – accommodation designed especially for them. Sonia decided that she didn't want to stay there. It would be a busy, noisy place filled with thousands of young people. The athletics events were always last at the Olympics, and Sonia felt it would be hard to be surrounded by people whose events were already finished and who could relax and have fun. She'd need early nights, rest and calm before her races – not a party atmosphere where others were already on holidays. So she got a place of her own away from all the noise and mayhem, and concentrated on keeping to her normal routine.

The heat for the 5000 metres was two days before the final. Sonia knew that a lot of her old foes weren't going to be running in the event – Fernanda Ribeiro, Julia Vaquero and Derartu Tulu had all decided against it, concentrating on the 10,000 metres instead.

She was drawn in the same heat as Swedish runner Sara Wedlund. Just like at the World Championship, Sara set the pace early on, hoping to lose everyone. Sonia had found it easy to beat her in Gothenburg. But now she struggled to catch up with her. She didn't have to win this race, just do enough to qualify for the final. But she felt that if she didn't win, she'd be making herself look weak in front of her rivals. So she dug deep and managed to finish in first place. She had won, and had shown everyone what she was capable of. But the effort had taken so much out of her – already she felt wrung out.

The day of the final came. Sonia went for a run

with her old friend Frank, out by the Olympic cycling venue. They weren't running fast, but Sonia didn't feel well. Suddenly she no longer believed in her own abilities. Her mind was a whirlwind of doubts and panic. She found herself rushing for the toilet, her tummy heaving.

'You'll be grand, Sonia,' Frank said, trying to reassure her.

'Ah yeah, I'm fine,' Sonia said.

But deep down, she knew she wasn't.

The race wasn't until the evening. Sonia and Kim went for a drive in the afternoon to pass the time. She ate her usual pre-race meal of fish and rice.

It was the chance she had dreamed of since she was a young girl, and she just didn't feel right. It was as if all the energy had been drained out of her. She could only hope that the atmosphere in the stadium – the Irish fans cheering her on, the bright lights, the crack of the starting gun – would be enough to carry her through.

The stadium was packed to the rafters – 83,000 people all watching the race, and all over the world millions more would be tuning in. In the vast crowd Sonia could see glimpses of green – Irish supporters in hats and t-shirts, waving their flags and shouting encouragement. Somewhere in there were her mam and dad, proud as punch of their daughter. It was a little piece of home in this huge venue.

They were off! Once again Sara Wedlund took the lead. Usually Sonia felt comfortable at the start of a race. Like she just needed to bide her time, put in the yards until it was time to make her move. Tonight she felt it was a struggle just to hang on. It wasn't as hot as it could have been in Atlanta, and there was a gentle breeze. But still Sonia was sweating buckets.

About halfway through the race, Sonia's friend Pauline Konga from Kenya had taken up the lead and was setting the pace. Sonia hung on grimly. Just a few laps more, she told herself. Just finish this race, and we can figure out what's wrong later.

The Irish team officials were getting more and more worried as they watched Sonia run. They could tell something wasn't right.

There had been times before when Sonia missed the crucial moment when the leaders broke away – when she failed to speed up at the right time. But tonight she didn't miss it. She just wasn't able to respond. Mentally, she reached down inside herself, trying to find that injection of pace that she needed. She had nothing there.

Suddenly the leading pack were well away from her. The gap that had opened up would be impossible to close. Sonia, the favourite to win the race, was in last place. She kept going, her mind in turmoil. Was there any point in carrying on? She knew she couldn't win or even come close. Should she save what little energy she had for the 1500 metres and hope that she would feel better on that day? She'd do one more lap, she told herself, and then see how she was.

All the Irish voices in the crowd had gone silent. Sonia caught sight of her own face on one of the screens over the huge Olympic stadium. She looked as dreadful as she felt.

Decision time. Two laps to go. Sonia turned off the track and ran down the exit tunnel. Her race was over.

In her head, Sonia thought she could go straight out of the stadium, escape the waiting journalists, and not have to speak to anyone but her family and coaches. But there were officials waiting for her, asking how she was, if she needed medical attention. Sonia wanted nothing more than to be left alone, but she allowed herself to be taken off to the medical room, thinking she would have a few minutes to get her head together.

She had just walked off the track of the biggest event she had ever done in her life. The world was watching. What on earth had she done? She couldn't get her head around it.

There was nothing she could say to the media. No way to make sense of it all. She quickly put on her t-shirt and leggings and found her family and Kim. They hugged her and reassured her that everything would be all right.

Sonia's dad spoke to the media. 'Nobody died,' he told them. 'Everyone will get up tomorrow and go to work as normal. It's only sport, and there'll be another day.'

It made Sonia feel better hearing her dad's words. She knew he was right. Even when it felt like her world had collapsed around her, it was only a race.

Later that night, Sonia and Kim ran home from the stadium together, talking over everything that had happened. Kim reminded her of all the support that was there for her in the stadium, and of all the hard work she had done to get to this point. Sonia was already starting to focus on the 1500 metres, sure that it could have a happier ending.

'NOBODY DIED'

Sonia tossed and turned that night, finding it impossible to go to sleep. The race kept playing on a loop in her head, over and over again. She had been the favourite for an Olympic gold medal and she hadn't finished the race. She couldn't help but feel that from now on she would think of her entire life as being divided into 'before Atlanta' and 'after Atlanta'.

But there was still the 1500 metres to come. A chance at redemption. She lay in bed next morning trying to think positive thoughts about the next race.

When she got up, there were so many people gathered in her house that it felt like an Irish wake.

She remembered her dad's words – 'Nobody died' – and smiled sadly to herself.

Sonia turned to what she always turned to in times of crisis – running. She pulled on her runners and went out for a twenty-five minute run, testing herself to see how she felt. She was OK. Not brilliant, but not terrible. The 1500 metres felt like something she could do.

The Olympic Council wanted her to do a press conference. Although the thought of speaking about what had gone wrong was very daunting, she felt that she owed it to all her supporters back home. She did her best to explain what had happened, but it was a struggle when she didn't really understand it herself. Afterwards she went out for lunch with her parents, grateful to have normal company.

Her parents had been her rock through this awful time. The night before, they'd gone out to a party in a pub called the Irish House. It was a sort of unofficial headquarters for the Irish in Atlanta. The O'Sullivans thought they would be there celebrating an Irish gold medal that night. Instead they had people coming up to them and saying how sorry they were that it hadn't worked out.

Frank went to the warm-up track with Sonia before the heats of the 1500 metres. He had always been there for her, like a big brother. He knew she would be feeling down, and he wanted to give her a bit of encouragement.

'You know you've got this in you, Sonia,' he said. 'You've beaten all these girls before. This race is yours for the taking.'

Sonia tried hard to believe him. She put on a brave face. 'Ah yeah, I'll be grand. Just need to get out there and qualify for the final, one step at a time!' In the effort of smiling and acting like everything was going to be OK she almost convinced herself as well as Frank.

If she could just get through this qualifying heat, she would have a few more days to recover from whatever it was that was wrong with her before the final.

But out there on the track, she still felt drained, as if her body was giving up on her. It was unbearably hot, and the sweat poured from her as she pumped her way around the track.

Sonia could only watch as, one by one, girls she had easily beaten before passed her out. She finished tenth, out of eleven runners.

Her Olympic Games were over.

CHAPTER TWENTY

RUN DOWN

For the next two weeks, Sonia cried herself to sleep every night. She couldn't get her head around the fact that her dream was shattered. Everything she had been working for for the last four years, since the heartbreak of Barcelona – just gone.

Sonia had always believed that the world saw her as strong. In control. Capable of anything. Now it was as if her armour had crumbled and her true weakness had been exposed for all to see. She felt completely vulnerable.

The worst thing was that she felt she only had herself to blame for what had happened. She had ignored all the warning signs from her body telling her she was running on empty. It was like when she was a teenager back home in Cobh, pretending not to be sick so her mother wouldn't stop her from going out running. Now she was an adult, and the only person she was fooling was herself.

Back home in London, letters came pouring in from Irish fans offering her sympathy and support. Sonia read through dozens and dozens of letters, in tears again at the kindness of these supporters. Her favourites were the ones she got from children, many of them with drawings attached. Some of them made her laugh. She did her best to write back to as many as she could, sending autograph cards. It made her feel good to be doing something nice.

But soon it was time to get back to training. Sonia put the pile of letters aside and got back to work. She needed to boost her confidence, and she only knew one way to do that – get out there and win a race.

Kim signed her up for a 3000-metre race. This felt like a good distance to tackle – it would be over much quicker than the 5000 metres, so she didn't have to keep up her top performance for as long.

She ran the race. She won. Confidence came

surging back, and Sonia immediately agreed to do the Grand Prix in Milan.

But her newfound recovery wasn't to last. She started struggling with running distances she usually found easy. Sonia just kept pushing herself, working harder and harder, refusing to accept that what she really needed was to take a break.

At last she went for some medical tests in the University of Limerick at the National Coaching and Training Centre, hoping to find some answers.

The doctor called Sonia into her room.

'Well, are you going to be able to fix me?' Sonia joked.

The doctor looked at her over her glasses. 'I'm afraid you're going to have to fix yourself,' she said seriously. 'You're completely run down, Sonia. You're not looking after yourself. You have a urinary tract infection, so we can give you antibiotics which should clear that up quickly. But really what you need to do is to rest, and eat well, and just mind yourself a bit.'

Sonia had hoped for some sort of magic solution to how she was feeling. Even though it was a strange thing to wish for, she would have liked to be able to say to people, 'This is why I didn't do well in Atlanta.' She didn't want to be told that it was as simple as being run down, that all she needed was to rest and look after herself a bit better.

The one good thing going on in her life was that she had become close to Nic Bideau. Nic was an agent and coach from Australia, who had worked with some of the best athletes in the world. He lived in the same crazy running world as Sonia and understood what she was going through. Soon their friendship blossomed into love.

But her running still wasn't right. At the World Championship in Athens she had another couple of races that she only wanted to forget. In the final of the 1500 metres she finished a disappointing eighth, and in the 5000 metres – the distance where she was the defending champion – she didn't even qualify for the final.

Finally Sonia realised the time had come to take a real break. She and Nic went on holidays to Sicily. The beautiful narrow cobblestoned streets weren't designed for running on. You could catch your foot in a stone and break your ankle. So, for the first time in as long as she could remember, Sonia didn't run. She lay in the sun soaking up its warmth. She had long lazy dinners, eating as much as she wanted. She went swimming in the sea, enjoying the feeling of the water. It was as if they had escaped from the real world, and it was wonderful.

CHAPTER TWENTY-ONE

A NEW PLAN

When it was time to get back to training, Sonia felt properly refreshed. She had a new coach called Alan Storey who designed new training sessions for her. For the first time she wasn't training at such a high intensity. Instead of coming home from sessions and needing to take an ice bath to recover, she was finishing the sessions with energy left to spare. She'd get back to the house and do the hoovering or mow the lawn.

It felt very strange. Sonia had been so used to giving everything to her running, to pushing and pushing herself until she was utterly exhausted, that she felt like she wasn't working hard enough now.

'How can I get to my best if I'm not training

harder?' she asked Alan. 'I'm not running as fast as I know I can.'

'Trust me,' said Alan. 'I've got a plan to get you back to your best. You know it wasn't working pushing yourself to the limits, right?'

'Right,' Sonia admitted.

'So we're going to do it my way for a while.'

Sonia gave in. She figured she had nothing to lose at this point.

That October, she ran in a 5000-metre road race and won easily. Suddenly she realised that the method was working. It was so tempting to push harder, see what she could really do. But she had a slight calf injury which forced her to take a few weeks off. Hard though it was not to be training, deep down she knew the rest would do her the world of good.

Sonia started spending more time in Australia. She loved life Down Under. Australia's stunning scenery made the perfect backdrop to running. With Nic and a big group of running friends, she spent some time in Falls Creek, a beautiful area 1500 metres above sea level, for altitude training. Altitude training was something a lot of athletes did to improve their fitness. Because the air was 'thinner' at that height above sea level, every breath delivered less oxygen to hard-working muscles than they needed. So the body would produce extra red blood cells to get the oxygen to the muscles faster, and this meant that on returning to sea level athletes would experience a boost to their fitness.

On their first session, Sonia threw herself right into it and ran up a huge hill with some of the group who had already done plenty of altitude training. Almost at once she realised her mistake. She had the classic symptoms of altitude sickness – a thumping head and nausea. Not a pleasant combination with running in the wind and rain.

But after a few sessions, Sonia began to adjust to running at altitude. She was excited to see what difference it would make to her fitness levels.

She spent four weeks in Falls Creek, sometimes training with the other athletes, sometimes on her own. It was a wonderful feeling running along high tracks where she was above the clouds.

Sundays were always her day for a long run by herself. She ran for miles through the countryside, feeling homesick for Cobh when she passed fields full of cows. It was a funny thing to be homesick for, those days when she would run through fields trying to avoid cow-pats!

CHAPTER TWENTY-TWO

MARRAKECH

Sonia's next goal was the World Cross Country Championship in Marrakech in Morocco that April. It was an event that held a special place in Irish people's hearts. John Treacy had won two titles in a row in the 1970s, and Ireland had taken an interest in it ever since.

After Athens, Alan had suggested to Sonia that this was a good event to aim for. It would bring her back to her old love of running on green grass through open spaces. Plus it was far enough away that it gave her a good stretch of recovery time.

Now the date was getting closer. The plan all along was that Sonia would run the short race at Marrakech – the 4km. Sonia rang Alan to talk about her training. They had a good chat about what she had been doing.

Just as she was about to say goodbye, Alan said casually, 'You know, the short race at the World Cross Country is the Mickey Mouse race. Everyone knows the long race is the real deal.'

Sonia was so surprised that she said nothing. All along they'd been planning for her to run the short race. Now Alan was telling her it was a 'Mickey Mouse' race – meaning it wasn't taken seriously by real athletes.

'Bye then! Talk soon!' Alan said.

Sonia stared at the phone, feeling a bit annoyed.

The idea that she should think about running the long race instead began to tug at Sonia's mind.

Sonia travelled to Marrakech with her old coach Kim. He organised for her to appear at a press conference. Sonia felt she had been out of touch with the media for a long time, spending so much of her time on her own. It really boosted her confidence to see all these journalists gathered together in a room to hear what she had to say. Suddenly she felt like a star again.

When they were finished, Sonia and Kim headed

out to the race course to go for a jog. The course was surrounded by olive groves, and people were rushing around getting everything ready for the races.

Some of the Irish journalists who had travelled to Marrakech found the hot weather oppressive. But Sonia was used to the heat after spending time in Australia.

By now Sonia was completely focused on the longer 8km race. Seeing the course in advance was always a help, especially with cross country, which could be unpredictable. She felt more prepared when she had a clear vision of where she would be running.

The day of the race arrived. Sonia felt a new sense of confidence surging through her as she made her way to the venue. She was quietly confident that she had prepared as well as possible. This might just be the comeback she was dreaming of.

Running cross country was so different from running at the track. Not only were there no lanes, there wasn't even a starting tape. In big races, Sonia was used to jockeying for position near the start line, making sure she wouldn't get boxed in. But here they literally were in boxes – wooden stalls marked the start of the race. Sonia felt a bit like a greyhound getting ready to be released!

They were off! A frantic mass of athletes pouring out of the wooden stalls, dust clouds flying up from under their feet. They started off at a hectic pace, the Kenyan athletes leading the way. Sonia tried to stay calm and focused. Sure enough, the pace soon slowed down, and Sonia felt more comfortable. Everyone was running along as if it was just a training session.

As the race went on, Sonia could see the athletes eyeing each other up, everyone waiting for someone else to make the first move. Sonia stuck to her plan – just keeping up with the leading pack, biding her time.

Tensions rose as they got to the last lap. Sooner or later, someone would have to pick up the pace.

All of a sudden Sonia realised that everyone around her was getting tired. Even better was the realisation that she wasn't. She could win this race if she just found that old injection of pace.

There were three of them in front as they approached the last 400 metres – Sonia, Paula Radcliffe of the UK and Gete Wami of Ethiopia. They were looking out for the officials who would direct them down the right route. But the officials sent them the wrong way! Paula hesitated and Gete almost stopped. But Sonia kept going. She had examined the course the day before and she knew she was running parallel to the correct route. More importantly, she knew there was a gap in the fence up ahead where she could get back onto the home straight.

Sonia accelerated, drawing away from the other two women. She was out in front now. No one was near her. She ran through the gap in the fence. The finish line was in sight.

'Just keep it up, keep it up,' she muttered to herself. She could see Kim waiting for her just across the finish line. No one between her and the world title.

She crossed the line. She had done it! She was the World Cross Country Champion!

Photographers crowded around. Journalists asked for quotes. Someone pushed an Irish flag into her hands. Officials tried to bring her here, there and everywhere.

Sonia was the centre of attention once more, and she loved it. All the fuss she had once found overwhelming was suddenly the best feeling in the world. After the disappointments of the last few years, victory was all the sweeter.

Sonia was still entered in the short race the next day. At the time it had been almost a fallback plan – if the 8km didn't go well, at least she still had a chance of winning a medal in the 4km.

Now she had her gold medal. She didn't need that second chance. But wouldn't it be just wonderful to win both races? She was in two minds, half thinking she wouldn't bother – half knowing she couldn't resist.

In all the madness after the race, Sonia's bag with her phone in it had gone missing. She'd spent ages looking for it, checking lost property, asking officials. But in a strange sort of way, she saw it as a sign. She wouldn't call Alan, or anyone else. She'd just make up her own mind.

Walking to the start line the next day, her phone

in her hand once more, she finally called Alan to tell him where she was.

'You're mad,' Alan sighed, knowing there was no stopping her now.

'Think of it like Wimbledon,' Sonia said. 'I've won the singles, now I'm entering the doubles. I've already won the main event. It'll be a bonus if I win this too.'

'I just don't want you to be upset if you lose,' Alan said. 'It'd be a shame to take the shine off yesterday.'

'I won't be upset,' Sonia assured him. 'But Alan? I'm not going to lose.'

She didn't lose.

A second gold medal around her neck, she rang Alan back, thrilled.

'Well done, Sonia,' Alan said. 'I'm just glad there's no mixed doubles!'

CHAPTER TWENTY-THREE

EUROPEAN CHAMPIONSHIPS, BUDAPEST

For Sonia, the double victory at the World Cross Country Championship was truly special. This time, she was determined to savour the moment. She thought back to the World Championship in 1995, when she'd won gold in the 5000 metres. She realised now that she hadn't celebrated that moment enough. Because she was expected to win, and expected herself to win, it was more a feeling of relief than joy.

She was older now, and knew that there were only so many chances in a running career that an athlete could reach the top. This time, she would treasure every second.

She flew to the United States for a meeting with a sportswear company. They had a huge banner up to greet her – 'Welcome Sonia O'Sullivan – World Cross Country Champion.' Sonia was grinning from ear to ear.

Back home in Ireland, Sonia didn't want to do the open-top bus style celebration she'd had before. She thought too of homecomings in Cobh, with a band playing and the square packed full with people wanting to celebrate her success. This time, she didn't want a fuss. She decided that the perfect way to celebrate was by doing a run from Cork to Cobh, as part of her charity work with the Guide Dogs for the Blind. She could wave to supporters along the side of the road.

She hadn't expected it to be such a huge event. So many people wanted to wave to her and to show her their support. Her arms were nearly dropping off by the time she reached her home town!

It was time to start thinking about the European

Championships. Every time she looked at the schedule, Sonia found herself drawn to the 10,000 metres. It was a distance she hadn't done before, but she felt like it would suit her. And because the race was first, she could still go for the 5000 metres too if she wanted to.

The Olympic champion, Fernanda Ribeiro, was running the 10,000. Sonia was excited at the thought of taking her on. They had run against each other so many times and Sonia knew she was a brilliant athlete. It would be quite a challenge to run against her over this new distance.

Some of her friends tried to discourage her.

'You know you have a problem with concentration even over shorter distances,' Kim told her. 'How do you think you're going to stay focused for a whole 10 k?'

Sonia knew he had a point, but she wanted to at least give it a go.

'I've got nothing to lose,' Sonia decided. 'It's half an hour out of my life!'

There were no heats for this event, just straight into the final for athletes who met the qualifying time.

Budapest was a beautiful city. Sonia enjoyed running along the river, crossing the historic bridges, taking in all the sights and sounds. Back at her hotel later, she lay down on her bed to rest and read the latest Harry Potter book.

When the day of the race came around, Sonia felt calm and in control. She only had one tactic in mind this time – just to keep up with the leaders for as long as possible. No more, no less.

The race started off slowly. Just four laps in, the athletes had split into two groups. Sonia was in the leading pack along with Fernanda, a Romanian girl called Lidia Simon, Paula Radcliffe of the UK and Olivera Jevtic from Yugoslavia. The Spanish girl, Julia Vaquero, managed to catch up with them. Already it was clear that the winners would come from this group.

Sonia kept waiting for one of the girls to pick up the pace. They all knew she had a strong final kick, so their best hope of winning was to tire her out early on. But the first half of the race was run in 16:08.35, not a fast time at all for runners at this level. Sonia's mind wandered a little bit. She felt more and more relaxed. Maybe they all thought her best days were behind her. Maybe they didn't believe she still had that fast finish! She stayed in third or fourth place, just keeping on keeping on.

At last, at 7000 metres, Julia Vaquero sped ahead. The other girls were quick to follow. Sonia lost her concentration for a moment and slipped a couple of places behind. But she snapped back into it and quickly made up the gap.

Sonia was still feeling comfortable, and she knew it must be showing in her face. That awful night in Atlanta she'd been covered in sweat, her features all clenched, the misery etched in every feature. Now it was completely different – and she knew both Fernanda and Paula would be able to see that too. It was only a matter of time before one of them attempted to burn her off.

It was Paula who made the first move. Sonia watched as she surged ahead, her head bobbing in her own unique style. But the others stayed with her.

Next Fernanda tried to break free. She took the lead and began mixing things up a bit by changing the pace, faster, then slower, then faster again.

Sonia didn't panic. It was easy to stay focused

when her race plan was so simple – just keep up with the leaders.

They were coming in to the last lap, and Fernanda was still in front, with Paula in second and Sonia third. Still Sonia waited, hanging on for that moment when she would bring her strongest asset, her final kick, into play.

With half a lap to go, it was time. For the first time in the whole race, Sonia took the lead. Surging past Fernanda and Paula, she felt invincible. This was her time. This was her race.

Strong and powerful, she raced down the home straight to finish three seconds ahead of Fernanda.

Sonia felt like a child again, jumping around and punching the air in delight. She had done it! Her first 10,000-metre race at a major tournament and she had won!

There was still the 5000 metres to go. Should she run it or not? People were advising her against it, telling her to just enjoy her victory. Sonia gave herself a bit of time to decide. She stayed away from the stadium but watched some of the races on television. The men's 10,000-metre champion, Dieter Baumann, ran in the 5000 metres and didn't do very well. Maybe her friends were right and she was better off just going home with the medal she'd already won.

But the temptation was too great. Studying the list of athletes who were entered in the race, Sonia saw nothing to fear. She felt she was as good as any of them – and hopefully better.

One of the girls, Gabriela Szabo, had featured in several of Sonia's races before. She had won the 5000 metres in Athens a year earlier, when Sonia, the defending champion, hadn't even made it to the final. Sonia wanted to test herself against her, see if she could beat her this time.

Sonia's mind was made up. She had to give it a go!

The 5000-metre race took place on a blustery Sunday afternoon. Once again, Sonia decided to keep things very simple. She wouldn't do anything more than keep up with the leaders. Just keep on keeping on, until it was late enough in the race that she could make her move.

The first lap was slow, but in the second lap Gabriela Szabo took the lead and increased the pace, splitting up the pack. Sonia was in the group of athletes at the front, along with Marta Dominguez and Annemari Sandell.

'You go in front now!' Gabriela urged Sonia. She was clearly feeling the stress of being in the lead.

Sonia ignored her. Gabriela had chosen to go in front and now she'd just have to deal with it. Sonia would never forget her first Olympic final in Barcelona, when she'd found herself stuck at the front of the pack too early and had seen her lead slip away.

They ran on. Every now and again, Gabriela would try to get Sonia to take the lead, but Sonia stayed where she was, running comfortably in second place right behind her. She could tell it was really annoying Gabriela, but that was just part of racing. Staying in control of what went on inside your head was just as important as what your legs were doing.

With 500 metres to go, Gabriela injected some more pace. It took a moment for it to register with Sonia that this was a real move, and by then she had slipped into fourth place. She had to work hard to catch up, but soon she was back just where she wanted to be, running right at Gabriela's shoulder. They were back to the same pattern – it was as if Gabriela was the prey and Sonia was the hunter, always behind her.

Gabriela was such a brilliant athlete. Sonia didn't want to make a move too soon and find that Gabriela would catch her again. This time she waited until the final bend before breaking free. Using that last bit of power that she had, she stretched her legs one last time and ran at full stretch down the final straight.

She had done it! She was the 10,000-metre champion and now the 5000-metre champion too. Elation surged through her whole being.

Later that evening, standing on top of the medal podium and hearing 'Amhrán na bhFiann' played in the stadium for the second time in four days, Sonia felt her heart was overflowing with joy. Through all those dark days when she thought she might never win another race, the vision of this moment was what had carried her through.

CHAPTER TWENTY-FOUR

CIARA

And then life changed again, moving in a completely new direction. Sonia was expecting her first baby. She and Nic were thrilled, looking forward with great excitement to the birth of their little one.

'You'll have to take it easy now, Sonia,' Mam told her, on a long distance call all the way to Australia. 'Look after yourself and my grandchild, won't you?'

Sonia didn't know how to take it easy. But she knew running would be a bit different for a while at least.

Back in London, she did sessions at the gym, careful not to push herself too hard. She found it strange walking home from the running track – it felt like such a long walk when she was used to running it much faster!

She rang her old friend Alison Wyeth, who she used to train with. Alison had recently had her first baby too, and she was able to give Sonia advice on training while pregnant. The Scottish athlete Liz McColgan had also been through it, and told Sonia what had worked for her. Liz had decided to stop training six weeks before she was due and just enjoyed the first proper rest for a long time. Eleven days after the baby arrived, she was back running.

Sonia was fit and healthy, and while she knew she wouldn't be signing up for any races for a while, she was able to keep running, cycling and swimming as long as she felt well.

Baby Ciara was born in a London hospital at two o'clock on a July morning. Sonia and Nic were besotted with their new little daughter. Nic rang Sonia's parents in Cobh to tell them the news.

It wasn't long before the news was all over the radio back home in Ireland. Sonia had no idea how the media had got hold of the story, but it seemed everyone was just so excited for her.

Having Ciara changed Sonia's outlook. She was

no longer the centre of her own world, because this tiny little baby was depending on her for everything. She was filled with love for this gorgeous little girl.

But one thing would never change for Sonia, and that was her urge to run. Her competitive streak was as strong as ever. She found herself thinking about Liz McColgan, who'd gone running eleven days after giving birth, and another athlete, Ingrid Kristiansen, ran after ten days. Ten days seemed completely doable to Sonia. So, with ten-day-old Ciara in her pram, Sonia pulled on her running shoes and went out for a gentle jog.

Even in the warm glow of new motherhood, Sonia was conscious of the Olympic Games in Sydney, just fourteen months away. She didn't want to lose everything she had worked for up until now. She knew it wouldn't be long before she'd be back to full training.

Life with baby Ciara took on a new pattern. A run on her own in the morning, and a walk in the evening with the baby in her pram. Sometimes these evening walks became runs too, and Sonia would race along, Ciara's little face beaming up at her from the pram. She seemed to enjoy the fast pace, bouncing along and taking in everything around her.

CHAPTER TWENTY-FIVE

THE ROAD TO SYDNEY

The end of the year marked the dawn of a new millennium. With their five-month-old baby tucked up in her cot, Sonia and Nic watched the fireworks from the balcony of their Melbourne apartment.

More importantly for Sonia, it was the start of an Olympic year. It would be her third appearance at the Olympic Games – and maybe her last. She was thirty now, and already approaching an age where athletes started to think about retiring. She felt this was her best chance to overcome the disappointments of Barcelona and Atlanta.

Her trophy cabinet was pleasantly full. World Championship medals, European Championship medals, World Cross Country medals – she had an impressive collection. But what she craved most of all was an Olympic medal, to count herself among the greats of Olympic history.

The countdown was on.

Early in the new year, Sonia, Nic and Ciara were off to Falls Creek once more. This year the area was full of athletes and all the conversation was about Olympic qualifying times. There was a real buzz about the place, with so many people gearing up for one of the biggest events of their lives.

Sonia hadn't made up her mind yet about what events she would take on. The European Championship in Budapest had been her first experience of 10,000 metres, and with Ciara's arrival in the meantime she hadn't been able to do another one. She decided she would keep her options open by making sure she had the qualifying times for both the 5000 and 10,000 metres.

By February, Sydney was already buzzing with preparations for the Olympics. Sonia could feel the energy and excitement in the city when she arrived for the Australian Nationals. She'd chosen this event to try to get her qualifying time.

The evening before her race, Sonia went for a stroll around the Olympic stadium. She got a good vibe from it – it seemed friendlier than Atlanta. She felt at home there.

She needed to run the 10,000 metres in under 32:20 to qualify for the Olympics. She managed 31:43. She felt fit and strong, and very happy to have qualification wrapped up early in the year.

Spring saw the family back in London, preparing for some of the European races. There were good days and bad days on the road to the Olympics. Sonia didn't beat herself up when results didn't go her way. They were all opportunities for learning – she ticked them off and moved on.

In training for Atlanta, she'd gone hell for leather, full on, running her body into the ground. This time she would be more careful. She had everything to play for.

The 10km road race in Milan was an important one on the calendar. Sonia had a clear goal in mind – she wanted to finish in under 31 minutes.

The day before, some of the athletes were taking a bit of time off to go and see Leonardo Da Vinci's famous painting, The Last Supper. Sonia decided to join in. The last time she had been to Milan she had seen nothing much beyond the race track. Now she wanted to take the opportunity to see one of the most important attractions in this famous city.

The painting took her breath away. She had seen it in books and on TV but nothing compared to the real thing. Standing gazing at Da Vinci's work, suddenly it seemed to Sonia that nothing in her life was so big or scary any more.

The day before the race, Sonia and her family had dinner with Derartu Tulu. Derartu, an Ethiopian runner, had a little girl who was twenty-one months old. She made a fuss over Ciara and she and Sonia exchanged stories about running and motherhood. It was nice to talk to someone who understood.

Derartu and Tegla Loroupe were the ones to beat in this race. Both were top quality runners, with Tegla being the best road runner in the world just then.

At one stage, Tegla had opened up a bit of a lead. Derartu caught up with Sonia.

'Come on Sonia, let's go!' she urged her.

Sonia felt flattered that Derartu was putting her

in the same category. She wanted to go with her, but she knew it was too soon for her to kick on. They were on cobblestones which Sonia really didn't enjoy running on. But when they got back on to the normal road surface she felt fine again.

She made her move, catching up with Derartu, who nodded her encouragement. She caught up with Tegla. She could tell that Tegla was tiring already, so she just stuck with her, waiting for the right moment. When she finally took the lead, Tegla had no response. Sonia crossed the line in first place, a second under her target time of 31 minutes.

It was the perfect boost she needed in the build-up to Sydney.

★ ★ ★

As the Olympic Games got closer, it was time for Sonia to make up her mind about what event she would run. It was almost like a game of poker, with some athletes dropping hints about their plans, and others keeping their cards close to their chests.

Sonia had enjoyed the 10,000 metres, but she knew that her difficulties staying focused over that distance would be the hardest part. She felt that the 5000 metres was her best chance of success.

Nic and Alan disagreed about how much training Sonia should be doing. It was the kind of thing that would have made Sonia feel very stressed in the past, but having Ciara around made it all seem a bit less important.

Just before the Olympics, Sonia and her family went to stay on South Stradbroke Island. Even though it was a flight away from Sydney, a long way up the coast, it was a popular choice with athletes, and the place was crowded with others who'd had the same idea. Sonia saw one familiar face after another on the running tracks and in the town.

Coming back to the island by boat one evening, she bumped into none other than her great rival Gabriela Szabo. There was no escape!

CHAPTER TWENTY-SIX

THE SYDNEY OLYMPICS

T he Games were on. Sonia and Nic rented a house in the Sydney suburbs. No one knew they were there. It was a quiet, sleepy neighbourhood, not far from beautiful beaches, and the perfect place to escape from the hyped-up atmosphere around the Olympic village.

Sonia won her heat in an easy time of 15:07. It was the fastest time of all those who'd qualified from the three heats, but she knew she'd have to run faster than that in the final.

Sonia went for her runs and played with Ciara in the garden, waiting for race day to roll around.

At last the day of the final arrived.

'Got everything?' Nic asked.

Sonia checked her bag for the thousandth time. Running vest and shorts, spikes, tracksuit, drinks, race number.

'Yep,' she said. 'Let's go!'

Driving through the streets of Sydney, knowing she was on her way to an Olympic final, was surreal. Sonia said goodbye to Nic and Ciara, checked in and began her preparations.

One thing Sonia always did before a race was to lie for ten minutes with her legs in the air. She had no idea why she did it, if there was any scientific reason it might help her to run better. All she knew was that she had done it before the World Student Games in Sheffield in her Villanova days. She'd won that race, so she'd been doing it ever since. Athletes were superstitious types. Another of Sonia's little quirks was that she always believed she ran faster in white runners.

From where she was lying Sonia could hear the roars and gasps of the crowds, and the crackly sound of the announcer speaking through the tannoy.

It was time to go. Sonia made her way to the warm-up track, where she was amazed to see her dad sitting in the stands.

'What are you doing here?' she asked him.

'Ah, sure, I had to come and see you off!' Dad said. He gave her a big hug. 'The very best of luck!'

Dad made his way into the stadium. Sonia grinned to herself. It was unbelievable the way he always managed to be right there at the important moments!

Ciara was bouncing around on the pole-vault mat, watched over by Nic. It gave Sonia a lift to see her bouncing away, happy and carefree. Ciara was the perfect distraction Sonia needed. A little reminder that whatever happened tonight, in her daughter's eyes she was already a hero.

An official called the athletes in from the warm-up track. Sonia felt the butterflies surging back into her tummy as she thought about what was ahead of her. In just fifteen minutes she could achieve her dream of winning an Olympic medal, or she could see her hopes smashed to pieces once more.

In the holding room, they all waited, eyeing one another up, wondering who would be leaving with a medal, and who would be going home empty-handed.

Then came the slow walk through the tunnel.

The tense final moments, just wanting the race to begin, wanting to run and run.

On the start line, the camera panned from one athlete to another as the stadium announcer called out their names. Sonia smiled and waved, knowing the whole world was watching.

Bang! They were off. At this moment in Atlanta, Sonia had been filled with negative thoughts, overcome by the occasion, dreading what could go wrong. She was amazed at how happy and comfortable she felt here in Sydney, like everything was falling into place. There was nowhere in the world she'd rather be.

But after just four laps, Sonia found herself behind. She didn't know how it had happened. Everyone had just picked up the pace and she hadn't kept up.

For two laps, she was behind the leading group.

'Don't panic,' she told herself fiercely. 'You can do this!'

The words of a book she'd read came back to her. *Do you want this?*

'Yes!' she vowed to herself. 'Yes, I do!'

It was easy to say those words while out training, while talking to her coach or to Nic. But here in this stadium, with millions watching all over the world, she really had to mean it. She had to give it everything she had, even if it ended in failure.

The pace slowed down a bit, and Sonia was back in it. She was just behind three Ethiopian runners who seemed to be arguing among themselves. Gete Wami wanted the others to move to let her through, and they weren't shifting.

They were going faster, faster. Sonia's lungs felt like they would burst. She couldn't go any faster. Could she? The momentum of the race seemed to be carrying her along.

Sonia felt that she was running harder than she had ever run in her life. The crowd were nothing but a blur to her now. Her whole world was this track, these other women running, running their hearts out, beside and behind and in front of her.

She watched Gete. She watched Gabriela. She waited for them to accelerate. She knew they were watching and waiting for her too.

Then suddenly from nowhere Irina Mikitenko from Germany took the lead. Sonia wasn't expecting her to be the one to make the move, but she and Gabriela went with her. They passed her.

Now it was just the two of them, out in front, just like in Budapest two years earlier. Sonia was on Gabriela's shoulder, stalking her once more.

They came to the final straight. Sonia dug deep, giving it everything she had. She fixed her eyes firmly on the yellow of Gabriela's Romanian singlet, pictured herself reeling her in.

But Gabriela showed no signs of tiring. Even with her famous last kick, Sonia couldn't catch her.

Gabriela crossed the finish line, Sonia just one stride behind her. She was second in the world. An Olympic silver medallist.

Just a quarter of a second separated Sonia from the gold medal. There was a time in her life when finishing second would have felt like losing. But Sonia hadn't just run from the start line. She felt like she had run all the way from Atlanta, from out of that dark, miserable time, all the way to an Olympic medal. She was over the moon.

Someone handed her an Irish flag. She draped it around her and ran down the home straight, rejoicing in the cheers and roars from the Irish fans.

Nic and Ciara and her dad were there, hugging her, exclaiming in delight at her triumph. The Irish team officials were thrilled, rushing up to offer their congratulations. Sonia was the first Irish female athlete to win an Olympic medal. She had just written her place in history.

CHAPTER TWENTY-SEVEN

RUNNING ON

Nothing could beat the feeling of winning an Olympic medal. Whatever else she did in her running career, or in her life, Sonia would always have that memory.

Over the next few years, Sonia tried new things. She began doing some marathon training, wanting to know if she had an aptitude for it. She competed for an Irish team in the World Cross Country Championship in Dublin in 2002, thrilled when they claimed the bronze medal.

What made it even more special was that her second daughter, Sophie, was just three months old at the time of the event. Once again Sonia had made a remarkable comeback.

At the European Championship in Munich that summer, Sonia won two silver medals in the 5000 and 10,000 metres. Her time in the 10,000 metres of 30:47.59 was a new Irish record. After a decade competing at the highest level, she was still in top form.

But she was getting older now, and she knew that her running career would soon be coming to a natural end. The only trouble was, what was a natural end for someone whose entire career had been made up of elite running? If you were a footballer, you might come on as a substitute more often than you started matches, or move down a league to a less demanding team. What did you do as a runner, when it was all down to you?

Before she knew it, it was time to start thinking about another Olympic Games. They would be held in Athens in 2004, and some part of Sonia longed to have one last shot at Olympic glory. Deep down she knew that nothing could be as good as her experience in Sydney – that she couldn't add anything to what she had achieved there. But the temptation to give it a go was too great.

Coming up to the Olympics, Sonia's form was

good. Her times weren't as fast as they had once been, but she still felt confident that, if things went right for her on the day, she was in with a chance.

But it wasn't to be. Just before the 5000-metre final, Sonia was struck down with a nasty dose of food poisoning. Still feeling weak and well below her normal fitness level, Sonia was determined to run in the final anyway. She didn't want to let down all those Irish fans who had travelled to Athens to watch her compete at the Olympics one last time.

Struggling around the track, Sonia's legs felt like lead. Her head was spinning and she felt sick.

As the race went on, she knew she had no chance of a medal. Close to the end, the leading bunch lapped her. It was a strange position to be in for a woman who had once been on top of the world.

But Sonia kept going. And something wonderful happened on that final lap. All around the stadium, people started cheering for Sonia, clapping and calling her name. They knew they were witnessing the last Olympic race of one of the greatest middle distance runners of their time.

A group of Ireland fans who had been high up in the stands moved down closer to the track, holding their flags high and roaring Sonia's name as loudly as ever.

Sonia got a lump in her throat. It was as if they were there to share in her heartache, just as they had been there to share in her joy.

She gritted her teeth and fought against the feelings of sickness. She kept going. She would see this race out until the end, carried along on the waves of support from those fans in green.

It was the perfect way to say goodbye.

CHAPTER TWENTY-EIGHT

IRELAND'S OLYMPIC HEROINE

The atmosphere was electric in Dublin city centre. The Olympic torch was on its way through Dublin for a special ceremony.

It was 2012 and the Olympic Games were due to be held in London. The Olympic torch was the symbol of the Games. It was the link between the ancient Olympic Games, started in Greece in 776 BC, and the modern Games. Several months before the Games, it was lit at Olympia, Greece, starting the torch relay. It would then be kept lit right up until the start of the Games, when it would light the Olympic cauldron in the opening ceremony. There it would burn throughout the Games.

In the run-up to the Olympics in London, the

flame would be taken around both Britain and Ireland in a special torch relay, giving ordinary people the chance to see this famous symbol. Earlier that morning the Irish Olympic boxers Michael Carruth and Wayne McCullough had passed the torch across the border. President Michael D. Higgins had received it in Howth. Others who got the chance to carry the flame included Ronnie Delany, the gold medallist at the 1956 Olympics, and Bridget Taylor, mother of boxer Katie Taylor who would compete for Ireland at the London Games.

Sonia was thrilled to be part of this amazing occasion. She had been chosen to complete the last stage of the torch relay in Dublin, and she knew it was a huge honour.

Travelling through the streets of Dublin on the special bus, Sonia couldn't believe the crowds. At one stage the Gardaí had to clear people out of the way to let the bus through!

When at last Bridget Taylor passed the torch to Sonia, she felt overwhelmed at the knowledge that she was part of the amazing history of this flame. She ran past the cheering and waving crowds who lined the streets all the way to Stephen's Green.

At the gates to Stephen's Green, Sonia was joined by her daughter Sophie, who ran with her to the enormous stage that had been erected especially for the occasion. With Sophie by her side, Sonia lit the cauldron. She was overcome with the significance of that moment, not just lighting the cauldron that had burned all through Olympic history, but passing the torch from one generation to the next.

It was an amazing feeling to stand up on stage and speak to the crowd, who were so happy to see her. Sonia spoke about the special place the Olympic torch had in sporting history and what it meant to the Irish athletes to be involved. She talked about the lift it would give those dedicated athletes, reminding them of what they were training for, and why all the hard work was worthwhile.

Sonia was to be Chef de Mission for Team Ireland for the London Olympics. This special title meant she was the team leader, guiding and mentoring the athletes who were competing at the Games. She was very excited to be playing such an important part.

She was retired from athletics now and no longer competed professionally. But running was still a huge part of her life. It had been strange at first to stop running to win races, and just run for the enjoyment of it, and to stay fit and healthy. But now she was happy to be able to do that.

She was often asked to take part in events to promote running, and she was always happy to be involved. She loved to see children taking up the sport she loved.

Sonia's old training spot of Bushy Park in London became home to a new phenomenon. First called the Bushy Park Time Trial, it later became parkrun – an event that would spread to many different countries, with millions of people taking part every Saturday morning. Sonia was delighted to be involved in the early stages. She set the women's record at the Bushy parkrun, which would stand for four years, making it the longest-standing record at any parkrun.

Sonia loved taking part in parkrun – whether in London, Australia, at home in Ireland, or wherever she travelled to. She loved helping to promote parkrun too, as she thought it was such a brilliant event for encouraging health and fitness. It wasn't only for elite runners – people of all ages and abilities could walk, jog or run the course together every Saturday morning. She was glad to play a part in encouraging people to take it up.

Running for fun and for fitness instead of to be the best was a whole new world for her, very different from what had gone before. But in its own way it was just as fulfilling.

CHAPTER TWENTY-NINE

PASSING ON THE TORCH

'**A**nd there in the green of Ireland is O'Sullivan … O'Sullivan is looking strong … She takes up a position in the middle of the group …'

In the stands at the Gyor Stadium, Sonia is a bundle of nerves. It is scary enough being out there on the track yourself, where at least you are in control of what you do. It is a whole other level of nerve-wracking to stand on the sidelines and watch your daughter compete.

It's the final of the 800 metres at the Under 18 European Championship, and Sophie O'Sullivan is holding her own against the fastest girls on the continent. The British runner, Keely Hodgkinson, is the favourite for this race. But Sophie is tracking close behind her as they approach the last 200 metres.

At the warm-up track earlier, Sophie was tense, feeling the pressure of this huge event. But when she came out onto the race track, Sonia's heart lifted to see her dancing along to the music, looking relaxed, ready to enjoy this occasion whatever it brought.

It has been a special few days, being here in Hungary as part of the Irish team. This is Sophie's first time running for Ireland. She didn't know any of the other athletes before. The family is based in Australia, and Sophie, still only sixteen, mostly runs with her school team. Here on the other side of the world, the Irish athletes have made her so welcome, and she's having a ball.

'And there's the bell – we're into the second lap.'

'Come on, Sophie!' Sonia screams as her daughter flies past her. 'Hang on! Don't go too soon!'

'And now O'Sullivan is coming around on the outside, she passes Stoj and De Connick … but Hodgkinson is holding her off …'

Sonia puts her face in her hands. She can't watch.

And she can't not watch. She is hopping from one foot to the other, sick with nerves as she sees Sophie giving it everything she has.

'And Hodgkinson is pulling away down the home straight … O'Sullivan is looking confident in second … De Connick tries to catch her, but O'Sullivan is too strong … Hodgkinson is first, O'Sullivan second, De Connick third.'

Sonia jumps in the air and cheers. A silver medal! What a wonderful result.

Thoughts come surging back of other tracks, other races. Winning the Irish Cross Country Championship when she was not much older than Sophie is now, and declaring her intention of running in the Olympics one day. Those four separate Olympic finals, the heartbreak and the glory. World Championship medals, European medals, thousands of fans roaring her name as she raced. Great memories, filled with emotion.

Sonia rushes down to the front of the stand as Sophie comes to meet her. She hugs her close, crying and laughing at the same time. 'Well done, Sophie! I'm so proud of you!'

Sophie is smiling from ear to ear. She can't believe

it.

The next day, Sonia, as a former European champion, has the honour of presenting the medals at the medal ceremony. She places the silver medal around Sophie's neck, her entire face lit up with a smile. Her heart is full to bursting.

Who knows where Sophie's journey will take her? Will she one day run in her mother's footsteps around the tracks at senior European finals? Across muddy fields and up steep hills in the World Cross Country Championships? In front of thousands of cheering fans in an Olympic stadium?

Sonia doesn't know, but here, in this moment, her girl is a European silver medallist, and that is happiness enough.

SONIA O'SULLIVAN'S
ACHIEVEMENTS

Represented Ireland at:

Four Olympic Games (Barcelona 1992, Atlanta 1996, Sydney 2000 and Athens 2004)

World Championships (1993, 1995, 1997, 2003)

European Championships (1990, 1994, 1998, 2002)

World Cross Country Championships (1992, 1997, 1998, 2000, 2001, 2002)

Medals Won:

World Championship 1993 – Silver Medal, 1500 metres

European Championship 1994 – Gold Medal, 3000 metres

World Championship 1995 – Gold Medal, 5000 metres

World Cross Country Championship 1998 – Two Gold Medals, 8km and 4km

European Championship 1998 – Two Gold Medals, 5000 metres and 10,000 metres

Olympic Games 2000 – Silver Medal, 5000 metres

European Championship 2002 – Two Silver Medals, 5000 metres and 10,000 metres

Records

Sonia set a 2000-metre world record of 5:25.36 in 1994. This record stood until 2017.

She still holds the Irish national record for every distance from 1000 metres to 10,000 metres.

Hall of Fame

In 2019 Sonia O'Sullivan was inducted into the Irish Athletics Hall of Fame.

ACKNOWLEDGEMENTS

First and foremost, thank you to Sonia O'Sullivan for kindly agreeing to let me tell her story, and for taking the time to answer my questions, read the manuscript and correct errors. Any mistakes that remain are my own.

Thank you to my amazing editor Helen Carr, whose cheerful encouragement and attention to detail are what every writer needs. Thank you to all the brilliant people at The O'Brien Press.

Thank you very much to Aidan, Rachel and Sarah Fitzmaurice for reading several early drafts and for all your ideas and support.

GREAT IRISH SPORTS STARS

ALSO AVAILABLE

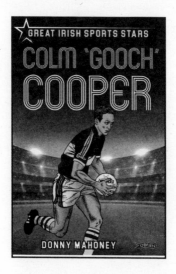

The Gaelic footballer who's won nearly every prize in the game:
Including 5 All-Irelands & 8 All-Stars

How a boy who everyone said wasn't big enough or strong
enough to wear the green and gold jersey of Kerry became one of
the greatest Gaelic footballers of all time.

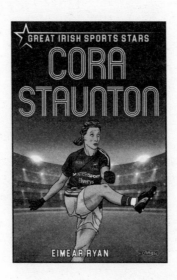

A Gaelic football hero in Mayo, a trailblazer in Aussie Rules
Winner of FOUR All-Irelands + ELEVEN All-Stars

The story of how a football-mad girl
became a living legend.